FAMILIES AND THE FUTURE

Children in Society Series

Edited by Stewart Asquith

Other titles:

Supporting Families

FAMILIES AND THE FUTURE

Edited by

Stewart Asquith and Anne Stafford

Series Editor: Stewart Asquith

HMSO: EDINBURGH

© Crown copyright
First published 1995

Applications for reproduction should be made to HMSO British Library
Cataloguing in Publication Data
A catalogue record for this book is available from the British Library

ISBN 0 11 495720 7

CONTENTS

FOREWORD

TOWARDS the end of 1993, the Royal Scottish Society for Prevention of Cruelty to Children and the Centre for the Study of the Child & Society, University of Glasgow, agreed to host an event to mark International Year of the Family in 1994. This became the Conference "Families and the Future" which involved invited speakers and delegates from the fields of Central and Local Government, academia, Law, the Churches, political parties and the voluntary sector. It was held in the Medical Conference Centre of Stirling Royal Infirmary on 13th and 14th September 1994.

At a time of unprecedented changes in families, and a public and increasingly polarised debate over family policy for the future, the Conference provided an opportunity to stand back and take stock of the current state of family policy and consider possible future developments. This book contains the speaker's presentations in full and a flavour of the discussions that they stimulated.

Children 1st (as the Royal Scottish Society for Prevention of Cruelty to Children is now known) and Centre for the Study of the Child & Society hope that this publication will be a contribution to current discussions and debates about family policy and stimulate some new ideas for the future.

Arthur M. M. Wood
    Chief Executive
    Children 1st

ACKNOWLEDGEMENTS

Our thanks are due to our contributors who, by and large, and with a little prompting met our very tight deadline. Connie Smith of Children 1st made the conference possible through her organisational and administrative skills and both organisations involved in hosting this conference owe her an enormous debt. She also however became more involved in helping produce this book than should have been expected of someone with many other duties to perform and we are both grateful to her for her help and patience in dealing with the manuscripts. From the outset, Alastair Holmes and Sue Hemmings encouraged the concept of the conference and the publication of the proceedings and we wish to thank them for their support, help and understanding.

Stewart Asquith and Anne Stafford

CONTRIBUTORS

STEWART ASQUITH

Stewart Asquith was appointed St Kentigern Professor for the Study of the Child and also Director of the Centre for the Study of the Child & Society at the University of Glasgow in 1992. He has worked previously in the Scottish Office, and in the Department of Criminology and the Department of Social Policy and Social Work at the University of Edinburgh.

ALISTAIR BURT M.P.

Alistair Burt M.P. was elected as MP for Bury North in 1983 and is currently Parliamentary Under Secretary of State for Social Security to where he was appointed in April 1992. He had served as Parliamentary Private Secretary to the Rt Hon Kenneth Baker MP from 1985 to 1990. He has been secretary to the Parliamentary Christian Fellowship since 1985. From 1987 to 1992 he was Chair of the Bow Group Industry Committee and from 1985 to 1988 Vice-Chair of the Tory Reform Group. Since 1990 he has been Vice-Chair of the Conservative European Affairs Back-bench Committee.

NIALL CAMPBELL

Niall Campbell has been the Under Secretary in the Social Work Services Group of the Scottish Office since 1989. He entered the Scottish Office in 1964 and has occupied various posts in The Scottish Office in the fields of education, land use planning, local government finance and transport. The Social Work Services Group is responsible for community care, child care, offender services and voluntary sector issues in the Scottish Office.

DAVID DONNISON

David Donnison is an Honorary Research Fellow at the Centre for Housing Research and Urban Studies at Glasgow University and Visiting Professor at the Local Government Centre at the Warwick Business School. Prior to this he was Professor of Town and Regional Planning and Chair of the Supplementary Benefits Commission. His books began with *The Neglected child and the Social Services* (1954) and the latest is *A Radical Agenda* (1991).

ROBIN GUTHRIE

Robin Guthrie was born in Cambridge in 1937. His first job was as Head of Cambridge House, the University settlement in South London (1962–1969). During this time he also taught in a Brixton comprehensive school, and studied social administration at the LSE. For the next seven years he was Social Development Officer in the Peterborough New Town Development Corporation (1969–1976). After four years in Social Work service and the Office of the Chief Scientist at the Department of Health and Social Security, he became Director of the Joseph Rowntree Memorial Trust (now the Joseph Rowntree Foundation) 1979–1988. He was appointed Chief Charity Commissioner in 1988, and moved to be Director of Social and Economic Affairs with the Council of Europe shortly after the passing of the Charities Act, 1992. In Strasbourg, Mr Guthrie carries responsibility for the inter-governmental programme of the Council of Europe in the following fields: Population and Demography, Health, Migration, Social Welfare, Social Security, Employment, Drugs Control, Food Additives and the European Pharmacopoeia.

MARY HARTNOLL

Mary Hartnoll was appointed Director of Social Work in Strathclyde Regional Council in June 1993 after serving as the Director in Grampian Region from 1978 to 1993. Prior to this she was Assistant and later Divisional Director in Berkshire County Council (1974 to 1977). She worked as a Child Care Officer in both Dorset County Council and Reading County Borough after completing her B.A. in Sociology at the University of London (1957–1960) and a Home Office Certificate in Child Care at Liverpool University (1960–1961). Mary Hartnoll was Secretary of the Association of Directors of Social Work from 1988 to 1993 and was also very actively involved in the Child Care Law Review.

LUDMILLA JORDANOVA

Ludmilla Jordanova is Professor of History at the University of York, she previously held posts at the Universities of Essex, Oxford and Cambridge. Her training has been in the natural sciences, history and philosophy of science, and art history and theory. She is interested in the cultural history of the family, especially in the eighteenth century, and in how "the family" is conceptualised. She has published articles on the history of the family, children, women and gender, and is particularly concerned with the use of visual sources.

KATHLEEN MARSHALL

Kathleen Marshall qualified as a solicitor in 1975 and worked initially in local government in Glasgow. She was Director of the Scottish Child Law Centre for five years, during which time she was heavily engaged in consideration of proposals for reform. In May 1992 she presented a submission to the Orkney Inquiry on behalf of the Scottish Child Law Centre. She is currently a freelance trainer and consultant on Scottish child law. She is, in addition, Visiting Professor to the School of Social Work at Glasgow Caledonian University, Gulbenkian Fellow in the Centre for the Study of the Child, University of Glasgow and a council member of the Children's Rights Development Unit – a UK wide charity aiming to promote and monitor the implementation of the UN Convention on the Rights of the Child.

ANNE STAFFORD

Anne Stafford has been Social Policy Research Officer with Children 1st for eight years. Previously she worked in the Department of Social Policy and Social Work at the University of Edinburgh. She was also author of *Trying Work*, a study of young people in Edinburgh.

FRAN WASOFF

Dr Fran Wasoff is a Senior Lecturer in Social Policy at the University of Edinburgh where she has worked since 1984. Her research interests are Gender and Social Policy and Law and Social Policy. She has carried out research on the financial consequences of divorce in Scotland and has also worked on the Child Support Reforms and the consequences for Family Law in Scotland. Prior to becoming a lecturer she worked for Citizens Advice Scotland and was the first co-ordinator of Scottish Women's Aid.

1

INTRODUCTION: FAMILIES AND THE FUTURE

Anne Stafford and Stewart Asquith

Introduction

TO mark the International Year of the Family, Children 1st (as The Royal Scottish Society for Prevention of Cruelty to Children is now known) and the Centre for the Study of the Child & Society at the University of Glasgow, jointly organised a Conference on the theme "Families and the Future". Held in the Medical Conference Centre at Stirling Royal Infirmary in September 1994, this book is a collection of the major papers delivered on the day.

The keynote speech outlining the Government perspective on the future of families and family policy was delivered by Alistair Burt MP, the Parliamentary Under-Secretary of State at the Department of Social Security. Family policy from a European perspective was presented by Robin Guthrie, Director of Social and Economic Affairs at the Council of Europe. Niall Campbell, the Parliamentary Under-Secretary, outlined a Scottish Office perspective on the changes in family life and the subsequent developments in social and other policy areas in Scotland. Professor Kathleen Marshall, Mary Hartnoll and Dr Fran Wasoff each discussed a major area of public life, (the Law, Social Work and the working of the new Child Support Agency Act) and examined the implications of these for recent major changes in the structure of the family. David Donnison addressed the important issue of family poverty and Professor Ludmilla Jordanova put some of the current thinking about the family into context by reflecting on the past.

The sixty or so specially invited delegates, all acknowledged experts in their field, were chosen on the basis of being in a position personally to influence thinking in relation to the family and family policy. They included senior representatives from Central Government, from Local Authority Departments of Social Work and Education, from the academic world, the Churches, political parties and the voluntary sector.

The Conference uniquely brought together this group of people, reflecting a wide range of topics, subject areas and "walks of life". It provided an invaluable opportunity to share information, engage in debate and for a frank exchange of views on the future for families and for family policy in Scotland.

The Family in a Scottish Context

It is clear that throughout Europe, the family is undergoing considerable social, demographic and ideological change. In that respect, the changes occurring in family life in Scotland parallel family change elsewhere. Though the contributions in this book are obviously not exclusively about Scottish issues, it was intended that what is happening in Scotland might be informed by consideration of developments elsewhere. Nevertheless, the changes in family life and the development of policies and practices in response have to be seen in the context of the social, legal and political institutions which have responsibility for families and family members.

The existence of very different social, educational and legal institutions in Scotland from those in England and Wales means that we have to avoid gross generalisations about family life and future initiatives directed at families which ignore important regional if not national differences. The fact that Scotland has a very different legal system which owes more to Roman law than English common law; an educational system with its roots in the European tradition of a broad based educational experience; and a juvenile justice system, shortly to be a quarter of a century old, which again is based on a philosophy derived from particularly French sounding notions of parenting as involving "education" and supporting family life – all these point to the need to accommodate cultural and historical specificity in our understanding of the development of policies which impinge on family life. More importantly, it also directs us to consider how future change in the way the state relates to families through the various policy and practice mechanisms have to take account of the historical legacy of successive governments and ideological trends.

Given the significance of a broader perspective in considering the implications of family change for policy development, it was very important that the contents of this book be informed both by a European and a historical perspective. In this way the myopia of considering local and familiar issues, in our case, of the family, as the only way of viewing the world can best be avoided. There is much to be gained from comparisons between countries and over time.

Nevertheless, it is also important to locate, albeit briefly, the issues discussed in this book in the context of key characteristics of family life in Scotland. Given the respective concerns of Children 1st and the Centre for the Study of the Child & Society, it will be no surprise that our efforts are directed more at the situation of children though this is not to diminish in any way the impact of change in family and social structure on other family members.

Social and Demographic Change

As is the case for children in most European countries, the lives of Scottish children have been affected significantly by major social and demographic changes. These include falling birth rates, the increase in the divorce rate, the numbers of children born outwith marriage and the numbers of children in Scotland living in poverty.

By the year 2011* there will be approximately 100,000 fewer children in Scotland over all age groups than in 1991 with children generally occupying a smaller proportion of the population, due not only to the falling birth rate but also to the increasing numbers of the elderly. For the UK as a whole, the average number of children per woman has also fallen to 1.8 in 1990 from 2.4 in 1971, reflecting the downward European trend.

But it is in relation to the changing nature of family structure that social and demographic changes most impact on children. In particular, in common with most other European countries, the proportion of children born outwith marriage is increasing and a rising divorce rate means that more and more children are living in one parent families. The rhetoric of the family is as a safe haven for children, yet the reality is that more and more children have to bear the emotional and financial costs of parental separation; and the reported numbers of cases of physical and sexual abuse within the family have risen each year.

The period between 1980 and 1991 graphically illustrates the changes in family life and in particular as they affect children. In 1990 27% of births in Scotland were to unmarried parents as compared with 10% in 1979, and in 1990 8% of all babies born were to mothers under 20, of whom 80% were unmarried. The marriage rate of the population dropped from 6.9 per 1000 in 1986 to 6.6 in 1991, with marriages taking place later in a relationship and fewer marriages involving those under 20. There is now a likelihood of 1 in 4 Scottish marriages ending in divorce with half of these involving a partner under 21. Moreover, younger children are increasingly likely to be affected by divorce or separation. Between 1980 and 1991, the total number of all children experiencing the divorce of parents fell by 9% but for those under 5, the total rose by 14% to 2253. Of all children involved in divorce proceedings in 1991, 24% were under five. Of all divorces, it is estimated that for 1 in 8 it is the second divorce for at least one of the partners. Thus a significant proportion of our children are faced with the emotional and other consequences of separation or divorce more than once.

Largely as a consequence of increasing divorce rates, the numbers of children in Scotland now living in one parent families has almost doubled; 44,000 children lived in families receiving one parent benefit in 1980, but 82,000 did so in 1991. One parent families now constitute 1 in 6 of all families in Scotland with dependent children and, not unexpectedly, most of these are headed by a lone female.

---

* This section is based on material in the white paper *Scotland's Children.*

What is also particularly disturbing is the high level of poverty experienced by many of Scotland's families and children. Recent estimates suggest that 440,000 (38%) of all children under 18 in Scotland live in poverty, i.e. in a household with below 50% of average income, and of these 135,000 are under five. The extent of poverty experienced by children in Scotland can be explained by reference to at least three factors, all of which are likely to take us well into the 21st century: the number of one parent families; unemployment of the head of the family; and low income.

The rising trend of unemployment during the 1980s, continuing into the 1990s, has compounded the problem, and has resulted in an increasing number of children living in families on benefit. Until such time as the economic situation alters, this will continue. For families in employment, the average weekly household income in Scotland has for the past decade been consistently lower than for the UK as a whole, standing at £261.02 compared with £303.84.

But increasing dependence of children and young people on their families will also be accelerated by the changing educational status of children. During the 1980s the numbers of pupils at secondary schools in Scotland fell sharply though it is expected that by the year 2009, the number will be 10% above the current figure of 294,000. By the turn of the century more pupils will fall into the certification net with a considerable increase in the proportion of pupils staying on after 16; 74% in 2000/1 compared with 57% in 1991/2. This will take Scotland into the higher band of staying-on rates maintained by a number of European countries. A greater proportion of pupils will also enter higher education.

The high unemployment rates for those 17- and 18-year-olds who left school at 16 coupled with the changes in the benefit system introduced in 1988 has also meant increasing dependency of this age group on their families.

The issue of poverty experienced by families raises broader questions not simply about what policies are developed by the state with regard to families and family members. The questions are more fundamental than that and require that consideration be given to the way in which resources and life chances are distributed in society. In short, the development of policies and practices that impact on families and children which ignore basic social inequalities in the distribution of wealth and life chances may offer little by way of attempts to ameliorate the conditions in which many families find themselves.

What we also have to throw into the equation though is the increasing concern at the harms inflicted within families on children and women. The current Scottish Office campaign on domestic violence is testimony to the experiences of many women and greater recognition given to the existence of domestic violence and its damaging effects, physical and emotional, on partners and children. Similarly, child sexual abuse and child abuse has come to increasingly occupy our attention and become a matter for concern. Between 1981 and 1991, the total number of referrals to Reporters to the Children's Hearings on offence grounds increased by 5%; the number of non-offence referrals however over the same period increased dramatically by a staggering 182%, mainly due to the increases in the cases where it was alleged the child referred was lacking parental care or was the victim of an offence. Now it is not the case that the increase in non-offence grounds can be attributed solely to an increase in the number of referrals involving child sexual abuse but what it does reflect is, at the very least, a heightened awareness of the ways in which many of our children experience the negative effects of family life.

Social Policy and the Family

The social and demographic changes in families also have to be seen in reference to major policy developments which directly impinge on family life. In particular, in Scotland in recent years a number of reports have appeared all of which address aspects of family life and the obligations of the state to particular family members. The *Report on Family Law* from the Scottish Law Commission; the *Report of the Inquiry into Child Care Policies in Fife* (the Kearney Report) from the Scottish Office; the *Report of the Inquiry into the Removal of Children from Home in Orkney in February 1991* (the Clyde Report) from the Scottish Office; the report *Another Kind of Home: a review of Residential Child Care* (the Skinner Report) from the Scottish Office; and the Scottish Office Consultation Document, *The Future of Adoption Law in Scotland* – all have a bearing on the lives of families and family members, particularly children.

The publication of the Scottish White Paper **Scotland's Children** in 1993 accommodated many of the recommendations in the various reports, bringing together different legal and policy developments in an integrated White Paper which provided a degree of optimism in Scotland that this would provide the basis for an integrated piece of legislation in the child care and child law field, fulfilling a similar function to that of the 1989 Children Act in England and Wales. (At the time of the conference, announcement of a Children's Bill for Scotland was eagerly awaited but it was to be another two months before a statement was made in the Queen's speech). The White Paper also however contained an explicit commitment to the embodiment in child care law of the principles of the United Nations Convention on the Rights of the Child which the United Kingdom had ratified (with certain reservations in relation to Scotland) in December 1992.

The UN Convention on the Rights of the Child is a potentially radical document which not only asks adults to rethink how we deal with our children but more importantly asks us to rethink the relationship between parents and their children, the nature of parental responsibility and the parental role. The philosophy on which the Convention is based is that children should have many of the rights available to adults and that they should not be exploited because of their age and vulnerability. In extending to children civil and political rights, the Convention is mistakenly taken to be only a charter for children to do what they want. Nothing could be further from the truth – the Convention contains an explicit statement on the rights and responsibilities of parents and also imposes obligations on signatory states to provide families and children with the wherewithal for healthy growth and development. Social, economic and cultural rights are also extended to children providing one of the most comprehensive statements of rights for children. The Scottish Office, through the White Paper *Scotland's Children,* have fully committed the development of child care law in Scotland to being based on the principles of the UN Convention and have also acknowledged the importance of the parenting role in whatever family structure children find themselves.

But the relationship between parents and their children and the nature of parenting has also been increasingly subjected to both the public and political gaze for other reasons. All too often, changes in policies and practices relating to children and families have come about as the direct result of some untoward incident involving children. The recent and tragic case of the murder and mutilation of the toddler James Bulger by two other young children, only just above the age of criminal responsibility themselves in England and Wales, amongst other things, has also forcibly placed parenting and family life on the political agenda. The relationship between children and their parents, parenting and the nature of family experiences and particularly the contribution of lone parent families, have become the focus of governmental attention in the attempt to explain many of society's ills, including crime. But, unfortunately, changes in policies towards children and their families have all too often developed out of some awful disaster – the Bulger case is one but we can also point to the significance of the O'Neill case, Maria Colwell, Jasmine Beckford and others in the development of policies relating to children which impact on family life.

What such developments and events identify clearly are different views not only on the role of parents and the appropriate form of family life but also on the contribution the family is seen to make in the production of society's ills. This is best illustrated by what might be referred to as the pessimistic view of family life in which many of the problems encountered in modern society can be attributed largely to the breakdown in family life and in particular the growth of one parent families.

On the other hand, the more optimistic view is that parents should be given greater recognition and appreciation for the job they do, often in the face of the severe hardship which results from family breakdown. Rather than moral censure, both moral and material support may be a more appropriate reaction. This sharply crystallises what was surely one of the key questions for the conference on which this book is based – how should we as individuals or as a society respond to the needs of families at a time when the family itself is going through great change.

Families and the Future

The family has been and remains a subject of intense interest to us all. Every one of us was born into a family and, for the most part, we go on to recreate another of our own. In his presentation to the conference, **David Donnison** argued "there is no more urgent topic in Britain today than the future of our families". The family is topical because it is clear that it is changing. And although historians tell us that the family through the ages has always been in a state of flux, they also confirm that the last forty years has been a time of unprecedented change, a change, as Donnison reminded us that is like nothing which has happened before in this century or in the previous one.

All of the chapters address these changes, some of which we have already outlined above. For **Alistair Burt MP**, these changes to the structure of the family have been unequivocally negative. For him, the family as an institution has become less stable, the ideal of the 'traditional' family under pressure. Quoting the British Household Panel study 1991–92, he claims that cohabiting couples are more than four times as likely to split up as married couples. Married relationships are, in his view, more stable, more likely to endure and more likely to provide the warmth and security a child so desperately needs. He argues for the status quo in employing a preferred conception of the family as one entailing lifelong commitment and marriage for preference.

Nevertheless, he is somewhat unequivocal in his analysis of the role the Government should play in relation to the family. Rather surprisingly he claims that families come in all shapes and sizes and the Government does not take a view on what an ideal family should be. The Government should not be the moral arbiter of society as many have a voice in the creation of a moral climate. The Government's fundamental duty, he argues, is to provide a legislative framework that underpins family relationships.

Other contributors do not disagree with assertions that children and families need stability. They disagree fundamentally however with Burt's analysis of how this can best be achieved. While agreeing that children need love, security and good care they do not believe the best way to achieve this is by harking back to a golden era in the past where families with two parents and children stay together for ever.

The taken-for-granted assumption on which the other contributions are based is that the nature of the family has changed and has changed for good; that the role of Government is to reflect and to take on board these changes, to introduce policies which support and accept the family in all its various new guises and disguises.

It is, of course, not all down to governments. There are macro explanations for some of these changes to family structure and fortunes. At a purely pragmatic level, as we have ourselves argued above, the declining birth rate has meant that throughout Europe populations are increasingly ageing. This has enormous implications for family policy.

David Donnison argues that from 1972 with the integration of the world economy, production has moved to the more stable of the low wage economies. The result is a decrease in demand for less skilled labour in the West. Wages become more unequal, with the lower third of the labour market falling further and further behind. They are increasingly becoming unemployed and unemployed for longer . He outlines the implications for society and for family structure of this increase in poverty and inequality.

There is now a polarisation, he argues. Families now tend to be either "job poor" households with no earners, or "job rich" households with two and more earners. Job poor households tend to be located in poor neighbourhoods and poverty in a neighbourhood where most people are poor is harder to bear than poverty in more fortunate areas. There are fewer jobs, fewer services, fewer and poorer charity shops, less transport, and fewer shops. There are increases in the number of children in public care, and on child protection registers, increased expulsions from school, declining literacy rates, increases in homeless young people, increased numbers of drug offenders, increases in reported crimes and in suicide rates among young people.

However, far from directly addressing the problems faced by poor families and ironing out some of their effects, the outcome of much Government policy in this area has been to ignore or even to exacerbate them.

Donnison went so far as to assert that the sharp increase in poverty and inequality is less an outcome of rising unemployment than the direct effect of changes in Government policy attributable to the tax and benefit system.

Fran Wasoff in her chapter on the Child Support Act is also interested in Government ideology and its impact on poor families as manifest in this new piece of legislation. She reminds us that the new legislation has not been an insubstantial change. In the words of the Social Security Select Committee, it is "one of the most far reaching social reforms to be made for 40 years". She claims "Its significance for family policy and for low income families in particular can hardly be over stated". Like David Donnison she claims that the Child Support Act is one of a number of measures along with the pension, tax and benefit system which, as a package, have had the effect of pushing responsibilities for families away from the State and back onto families. Rather than providing support for poor families, the Act has in many cases added to their burden. Far from operating to improve the situation for some of the poorer children and families in the country, most of the money raised by the Child Support Agency from absent fathers of children living with lone parents has gone straight to the Treasury and is deducted pound for pound from the benefit of the parent with care. Far from the Government introducing a package of reforms to tackle child poverty and to support single parents and help them out of the 'poverty trap', "We have seen a set of child support reforms that is greedy, cynical, and hypocritical, has not improved support for families in need... all in the name of rolling back the State".

Mary Hartnoll too is concerned with Government responses to family problems. She also asserts that Government policy in this area has emphasised parental responsibility and market forces. She points out that there have been increasing restraints on Social Services and on their ability to support families at a time when there is increased need. In her paper she goes on to outline what public policy changes are now necessary to support families if Social Work is to have a chance.

The argument that Government policy needs to take account of changes in the family, diverse family types and complex reconstituted families, is reinforced. For example, she claims that Social Work has depended and still depends on the traditional role of women as carers. However, fewer and fewer women across Northern Europe remain simply carers with the number of women in paid work rising. Women now make up 60% of the work-force in the UK and Alistair Burt himself points out that women are expected to account for 80% of the labour force by 2006.

Yet Government policy has done little to recognise this and to help women combine employment with child care or with caring for the elderly and it has important implications for Social Work. Increasing poverty and inequality have also had implications for, and put pressure on, Social Work. More children are in public care and there are many more on the threshold of care needing support. Mary Hartnoll warns that social work cannot and should not take on the task of resolving problems of poverty in families. That responsibility lies elsewhere.

Kathleen Marshall looks forward to the passing of the Children (Scotland) Act and considers the role of the law in Scotland in relation to the new configurations of the family. For example, the Scottish Law Commission's Report on Family Law (May 1992) grappled with the implications of changing family structures. One example of this is in her examination of proposals in that report which deal with co-habitation and the many legal dilemmas this poses. She also looks at the issue of the increasing value placed internationally on the rights of children which has led the Commission to ponder on how these values could best be expressed in law.

She discusses how the debates about a possible new Children Bill for Scotland [two months after the conference on which this book is based, a Children (Scotland) Bill was introduced on 24th November 1994] have struggled to identify the optimum point of balance between respect for the responsibilities and rights of parents and the needs and rights of children who may require protection. All of this, she claims, means that "the State has dug the first turf in the process of undermining the family as previously constituted."

Robin Guthrie, the Director of Economic and Social Affairs at the Council of Europe, outlines what is happening there to encourage member states to accommodate their own national laws and practices and to bring them closer to the ideal of coherent and integrated family policies.

He puts forward some ideals on which the principles of such a policy could be based:

> "to create the circumstances for the establishment of a family unit in which the individual can develop in safety, solidarity, self respect and with respect for fundamental rights on the basis of legal, social, cultural and economic criteria and taking account of the special needs of the different types of families and the different stages of family life..."

He also outlines key principles which could underpin a possible European family policy:

- Public authorities should ensure that a framework exists which favours the well-being and autonomy of families, with appropriate day care, medical, social, educational and cultural services.

- The plurality of family structures must be recognised and their specific needs acknowledged.

- The family should be the place where the rights of the different family members are equally taken into account.

- It is important to recognise that governments have a particular responsibility to protect families in periods of economic crisis and to take preventive measures to reduce the numbers of families living in poverty.

- Families should be able to participate in community life; not to be isolated but to be part of the mainstream of community life and decision making, and indeed of political influence.

The United Kingdom, and Scotland too, would do well to carefully note the values which might underpin future European Policy and Legislation in this area.

The Family: Everyone's Responsibility

Many of the contributions to this volume challenge the ideology of the present Government which is committed to reducing government responsibility for families and putting it back onto families themselves – often onto some of the most vulnerable families. Most of the papers firmly reflect the belief that children and families and what happens to them is the responsibility of everyone.

In relation to the Child Support Agency, Fran Wasoff views the problem as one in which the financial burden of child care is seen more as a private matter than as a shared social responsibility in which we all have a stake, making divorce and the breakdown of relationships more of a private trouble. The responsibility for child support is, in her opinion, certainly a joint one but involves society as well and not only the parents.

Elsewhere, Penelope Leach too has argued that children are everyone's responsibility:

"...whatever its merits, the old assumption that the family would meet all the needs of its own children outside formal school and that it should do so without any outside help as 'interference' is no longer tenable." (Leach 1994, p4.)

and,

"We have to recognise children as separate individuals in their own right, recognise they have needs, acknowledge the right to have those rights met and accept that while it may be the daily job of families to meet those rights, it is the job of the State to guarantee that right." (Leach 1994, p5.)

Children and families are too important to be thrown back solely on their own resources or left to the vagaries of the market. It is the role of governments to underpin families and family relationships, and to do so actively. The support offered needs to be extended and flexible in recognition that a pluralistic society like ours needs to accommodate and provide for a wide range of complex and reconstituted family configurations.

It is ironic perhaps that the last word in a book of papers given to a conference on the future of the family should go to an historian. **Ludmilla Jordanova** in her paper reminds us that it is important not to get stuck in our own taken-for-granted ideas of the family as these are a relatively recent phenomenon:

"Our current assumptions about family life seem so common-sensical, they have become so thoroughly domesticated, that getting a critical distance from them is almost impossible."

She tells us that:

"...it was only during the 18th century that the naturalness of the family, the idea that it was nature's most basic solid unit, was first systematically asserted and explored."

Today and in the past, intense emotional investment in the term 'family' means the term family can be used in quite emotive ways. There is potential in the term to suggest a norm to which to conform – to evoke a notion of idealised happiness and create a strong sense of what an ideal family is, through negative definition (in the past the negative object was the prostitute).

She herself draws parallels with recent attempts to idealise certain kinds of motherhood and to demonise others:

"We know how rigid and constraining notions of family have been in the past, which is the first step towards their not being in the future."

The profile of the family presented in this book is, very briefly, one in which the traditional notion of the family is difficult to sustain; the family may not be the haven of safety often assumed for many family members; there is increasing dependence on the family at a time when many families, through unemployment, poverty and the lack of support, may be least able to meet the demands of that dependency; and there is an apparent growing divide between the richer and the poorer sections of the community, charted throughout a number of European countries. Moreover, the move towards rights for children does have serious implications for the family and the relationships between key family members – especially parents and their children.

It is clear that, at this point in time, a transitional period is being gone through in which the roles and status of family members are being re-drawn and redefined in such a way as to challenge cherished notions of, for example, what it is to be a parent, without offering clear alternatives for consideration. Similarly, the role of the state in providing assistance to families and family members is also being questioned. But current concern about the family cannot be seen as simply being about the breakdown of family life. Rather it has to be seen as providing both the basis for a fundamental reappraisal of the very notion of the family; how governments respond to the needs of families at a time of change and the way in which social and economic opportunities are distributed.

References

Clyde Report (1992) *Report of the Inquiry into the Removal of Children from Orkney in February 1991*. Edinburgh: HMSO.

General Assembly of the United Nations (1989) *The Convention on the Rights of the Child* (1992).

Kearney Report (1992) *The Report of the Inquiry into Child Care Policies in Fife*. Edinburgh: HMSO.

Leach, P. (1994) *Functioning Families*. Paper presented to Family Mediation Scotland Conference, September 29th.

Review of Child Care Law in Scotland (1990). The Scottish Office.

Scottish Law Commission (1992) *Report on Family Law*. Edinburgh: HMSO.

Scottish Office (1993) *Scotland's Children – Proposals for Child Care Policy and Law*. White Paper. Edinburgh: HMSO.

Scottish Office (1993) *The Future of Adoption Law in Scotland*. Consultation Paper issued by the Social Work Services Group, Edinburgh.

2

FAMILIES AND THE FUTURE: AN OVERVIEW

Alistair Burt

Introduction

IT is quite right that we should be having this discussion on "Families and the Future" – there are many questions to be asked. But I hope that you are not expecting me to come up with all the answers. Like all of you here today I have hopes for the future – but I cannot pretend to possess powers of crystal ball gazing.

Very few issues in contemporary society have been the subject of such scrutiny as "the family". Such intense interest as we have seen over recent months reflects not only people's obvious interest in a topic of everyday relevance to themselves, but also their unease that something, somewhere, is not right.

I see the opportunity presented by the International Year of the Family to add to such discussion and debate. Family issues in modern society, anywhere in the western developed world, are complex and demand serious consideration.

Family Structure

The family is so important because it is the place where children learn to live in and contribute to society. It is where the individual first learns not only the aspiration of full personal development but also the constraints and responsibilities of living with others. If the individual does not develop all available talents and does not have the opportunity to do so, it is a life potentially unfulfilled. But equally, if the individual does not learn in the most natural of environments what it is like to live and work with and for others, and learn the limits of self, then we will all be the poorer. I see no contradiction in the encouragement of strong and secure individuals who will in turn contribute to the structure of society and community, for both have equal importance in modern life.

The ideal of the "traditional" family is under pressure from the reality of family life today. We all know that typical family structure is changing over time. Although two parent families are still the norm there have been tremendous changes over recent years. Change need not always be bad, but recent changes have made the family a less stable environment, a less secure place to raise a child. Stability is important in a child's life and stability is provided by the strength of the parents' relationship.

Research shows that instability is bad for children and that their development can be harmed by the break-up of their parents' relationship. If we are looking for stability then I believe we are looking seriously at life-long commitment and marriage for preference, as statistics suggest that married relationships are more stable, more likely to endure and more likely to provide the warmth and security that a child so desperately needs. The Economic and Social Research Council has recently issued a summary of some of the results from the British Household Panel Study 1991–92. One of their findings was that cohabiting couples were more than four times as likely to split up as married couples.

The type of changes in family structure that are most obvious at the moment are:

- An increase in divorce – more than 1 in 3 marriages end in divorce – a huge toll of human suffering of concern to us all. The annual number of petitions for divorce has doubled since 1971, whilst the number of marriages has fallen by a fifth.

- An increase in living together outside marriage – between 1979 and 1991, the proportion of non-married women who were co-habiting more than doubled from 11 per cent to 23 per cent.

- A growth of one parent families – there has been a vast increase in the number of lone parents. Twenty years ago there were just over half a million lone parents bringing up children – today, there are 1.3 million bringing up over 2 million children.

- The number of single lone parents increased from 150,000 in 1981 to 430,000 in 1991 (provisional figure).

- The number of divorced or separated lone parents increased from 500,000 in 1981 to 670,000 in 1991 (provisional figure).

- But the fastest growing group is the single never married lone mothers. About a third of lone parents on Income Support started out as teenage lone parents.

But it would be wrong to concentrate exclusively on negative statistics because:

- Marriage is still very popular – two out of three married couples stay united.

- Many people who divorce marry again, suggesting that the belief or hope in marriage and in families remains strong.

- The rise in the number of joint registrations of children outside marriage is increasing.

- The majority of parents bring up their children in united families.

- Most children, whether or not from broken homes, grow up to be responsible, law-abiding citizens.

But there clearly are serious social and personal problems arising from the disruption of family life. We cannot ignore them.

Government's View Of The Family

The Government's fundamental duty is to provide a legislative framework that underpins family relationships. Our programme of enlightened family law reform – the Children Act 1989, the Adoption White Paper, our proposals on divorce law and mediation – does just that. Our reform of public services in health and community care, in education, in housing and in social security has put families in the driving seat. Above all, we must acknowledge and respect the privacy of family life and reinforce parental responsibility.

What is an ideal family

Families come in all shapes and sizes. The Government does not take a view on what the ideal family should be. We all have views about the ideal family although these will vary according to our culture and background. I do not want to exclude anybody or any type of family by proposing a narrow definition. Patterns of work and social life are changing and with these changes so does the family. But families still matter.

I mentioned my own personal views before that marriage is most important. Of course there are loving and caring, committed, stable relationships between partners who are not married, but recent studies have suggested that couples who lived together before marriage were more than twice as likely to experience divorce or separation within 15 years of marriage as couples who did not. The decline of marriage as an institution and the increase in cohabitation are to be regretted if it results in more separations and in more relationships breaking up.

But while there are increasing challenges to stability, it is right to pay tribute to the tremendous achievements of family life in the 90s. We are too ready to react to the inadequacies of some aspects of modern family life, too rarely highlighting the achievements.

There is a danger that society is too ready to condemn a minority of parents; too slow to praise that great majority of parents who discharge their responsibilities well. But while challenging aspects of life that concern us

17

and need change we can also recognise success. We need to celebrate the strengths of families, as well as facing the weaknesses.

It is the sense of continuity provided by families and parents which is important, rather than prescribing the precise shape and structure of the ideal family. And that continuity is ultimately more important than material wealth. A family can be poor. It can be disadvantaged. It can be hedged in by adversity. But it can still provide a stable and coherent upbringing for our children. The greatest disservice which we can do to our children is to aim too low or expect too little, either of ourselves or of them.

It is right to be concerned for those in the greatest difficulty, but this can obscure the realities of life of the majority of people in this country. The vast majority of people grow up in a happy family environment, cared for by a loving mother and father, they enjoy school, do well and leave with some academic qualification – over 90% of children obtained graded results in GCSE, GCE, CSE or SCE. In 1992 almost a million children were members of youth clubs and more than a million youngsters were in the Cubs, Brownies, Boy Scouts or Girl Guides. They grow up to be law-abiding citizens, take up employment and in due course they themselves will marry. The headlines bring to our attention every young person that goes wrong but there is no celebration of the millions that turn out right and having learned good family values carry them forward into the community.

But we do have to deal with the realities of the modern family. It is right to seek to live up to ideals and high standards, but it is unrealistic to hold up an ideal of marriage and pretend that somehow, with spit, polish and a bit of character we can all achieve a perfect state of marital harmony. Marriages reflect the frail human parties to them, and, whatever our situation in life, our marriages are most likely to be a mixture of good and bad, stress and strain, joy and success, mistakes and forgiveness.

What role should Government play in these discussions? Is Government to be the moral arbiter of society? Plainly, No. The morality of a nation is conditioned by many voices and aspects of behaviour. The church, broadcasters and opinion formers, the written and spoken word reflecting the culture of the day, everyday activity of people – all have a voice in the creation of a moral climate.

Individuals are responsible for their own actions and must accept the consequences. The proper role of the family is to provide the environment where that responsibility can be learned and turned to good effect.

It is absolutely right for Government to be neutral in relation to consenting adult private behaviour. But the Government does have a role where there is an impact on others, particularly children. It is not always the same role. Sometimes it is to intervene directly by legislation, or to provide services to support the casualties of family break up. Sometimes it is a quite different role in advising and warning society of the consequences of private behaviour, where change must wait for a response from people themselves and legislative efforts alone are ineffective.

Issues – Now And In The Future

Separation

There is some degree of mythology regarding the 'golden age' when multi-generational families lived together. In Victorian times, for example, the family was a less permanent institution simply because people lived less long. The loss of a child, or even several children, was commonplace.

It not unusual now to see three or even four generation families – a result of an ageing population. We have to recognise the mutual support which exists within families. Grandparents help their children's children. Families care for their elderly or disabled relatives.

Of course families can become separated – for example when young people leave home or when elderly relatives can no longer be cared for by relatives. This is not wrong in itself providing that a mere physical separation does not break the bonds that should tie a family together. It is the responsibility of the family to work at staying in touch, to make an effort to remain in contact and ensure that a separation does not lead to bad consequences like neglect and loneliness and in this modern communications can help.

The elderly

It is undoubtedly the case that modern transport systems and commuting patterns have allowed family members to live far away from their traditional 'base' and that lower car-use by older people means that they rely increasingly on the goodwill of friends and relatives to visit them. Economic changes, too, can create migration of working people, leaving behind older relatives who may have grown accustomed to having their children and grandchildren nearby.

It should not be assumed that individuals living alone are necessarily also lonely. Those family members that can be on hand should help share the responsibilities and assist the elderly to live independently. Where this is not possible a greater responsibility will fall on the community to provide care. It is important that friends and neighbours provide support wherever this is feasible and we should not forget the selfless work of this kind that goes on throughout the country.

Many older people move into sheltered housing, residential care or nursing home care when they become too frail to manage at home. In some areas, particularly rural communities and inner city districts, this may require a move of some considerable distance from where they live. It is crucial that the assessment of individual need and the choice of residency/tenancy takes account of the network of relatives and friends. Equally it is important for the staff in care establishments and sheltered housing to actively encourage visits by relatives and to facilitate these in ways that respond to individual circumstances.

Youngsters

Young people of 16 or 17 years are at a crucial stage of their development into fully responsible adults and the support of their parents is important in helping these young people through what can be a difficult stage in anyone's life. I believe it is generally beneficial for people to remain living at home during these formative years.

Young people without a job are given the positive choice of either remaining in education or undertaking Youth Training. In both cases, the Government provides financial support to the family, through Child Benefit and continuing Income Support to the parents where the child chooses education, and through a training allowance to the child where Youth Training is preferred.

Of course, regrettably, some young people have to live away from home. The Government recognises this and provides extra assistance in Income Support and Housing Benefit both of which are paid at the higher 18–24-year-old rate.

Poverty

It is impossible to separate relationships from economic issues. As the world entered recession unemployment increased here and abroad and many families felt the pressures that result from the lack of work and having to manage on a low income. Neither are we in the UK alone in facing a change in the pattern of work away from other industries with fixed employment patterns to newer ones with less certainty of full-time employment until retirement. Such changes produce obvious and distressing pressures. People who at particular times in their lives are not able to support themselves should receive help from the State. This will include pensioners, the sick, disabled people, the unemployed and lone parents. Income Support provides a safety net for those whose resources are not adequate to meet their basic needs, but the best way to improve the living standards of families is to allow those who can to take up employment, and provide for themselves. We have tried to do this by making it more worthwhile for those who want to work to be able to do so.

Real take home pay is the best measure of living standards. It has increased 40% for couples with two children since in 1979.

A tax concession that was introduced in the 1990 Budget has encouraged employer-managed day-care for children. More employers are now interested in day-care and may decide to subsidise such costs because there is a business case for doing so. This is part of a practical policy to support working families – one which has also seen the growth of places in day nurseries and with childminders.

For families on low incomes, benefits as well as tax are of key importance. Since 1988 the Government has provided over £1 billion of extra help for families with children.

Changing Patterns Of Work

Benefit in work – the role of incentives

Social Security benefits and the incentives structure they provide can play a significant role in influencing labour market behaviour particularly at that crucial boundary, the decision to move from unemployment into work. The 1988 benefit reforms improved the situation by helping to develop an income-related benefit system designed to maximise work incentives by providing a coherent system that ensures that people are almost always better off in work.

Let me explain in very broad terms how the Government supports families.

Government assistance

We believe that the best way to improve the well-being and living standards of families is to make it more worthwhile for those who can to take up employment, and to provide for themselves. Improving incentives to work is more than just a matter of reducing the burden on the state. It is an essential element of human nature and human dignity to want, wherever possible, to live an independent life, to want to stand on one's own two feet and to want to provide for one's own family.

Family Credit

Family Credit is an example of how we have adapted our benefits for families to the needs of the 1990's and beyond. Family Credit, as an income-related benefit, can be targeted on families with low incomes who need greater assistance to bring up their children.

We have demonstrated our commitment to helping families back to work by providing help with child care costs from October this year. 150,000 working families will benefit by up to £28 a week in Family Credit. We believe families are better off in work than receiving Income Support and we expect 50,000 to take up work and be better off as a direct result of this change.

CHB

Another 'family benefit' is Child Benefit – the one benefit with near 100% take-up. It goes to every family in the land and is paid for every child – about 12 and a half million of them. Receipt of Child Benefit is the door to child allowances in almost all other benefits.

Child Benefit was phased in between 1977 and 1979 replacing Child Tax Allowances and Family Allowances. In our manifesto we pledged to uprate CHB in line with prices. We have stuck to that pledge. A typical two-child family now receives £18.45 a week tax-free. This rates in the top three in the EC.

Child Support Agency

In addition to measures such as the new Child Care Disregard there are other initiatives which will do much to help women play a full role in the labour market. Not least of these is the introduction of the Child Support Agency, which aims to ensure that parents, where they can afford to do so, meet their responsibility to provide for their children.

In the past we have seen a steady decline in the amounts and incidence of payments of child support maintenance, which has resulted in an increasing proportion of lone parents being forced onto state benefits. Many such parents tell us that they want to work and the new child support scheme will contribute significantly to the freedom of choice available to many women. Regular maintenance will mean that they no longer feel tied to the state.

Changing role of women

Government recognises that women are a major force in the labour market and the trend over many years has been for an increasing number of women with children to have a job.

Marital status used to be most important indication of women's economic activity – this is no longer the case. In total there are now more women in work in the UK than any other EC country, except Denmark.

These trends are set to continue and women are expected to account for just over 80 per cent of the labour force growth by the year 2006. The greatest projected growth is among mothers aged between 25 and 44. This has important implications for employers who will need to adapt their working practices to ensure they are "family friendly".

The former Secretary of State for Employment, David Hunt, in launching an initiative in conjunction with the Equal Opportunities Commission entitled "Fair Play" said:

"Removing barriers to women's progress is vital for the UK and every European nation, if we are to be truly competitive. I am confident that the arrangements we are putting in place will lead very quickly to new projects and ideas. We must make full use of the talents of all of our people. Now that women make up 46% of the workforce, we have to remove all obstacles to ensure proper recognition of their abilities."

Family impact of women returning to work

The choice of whether to return to work or remain at home full time is an individual one. A working woman will provide for her children in a different way from one who stays at home. Both child and mother can gain confidence and enrichment from the educational and social experiences of nursery and work.

Child care

The return of women to work creates a demand for child care and the case is often made for Government to provide free child care for all those who need it. But we believe it would be wrong to use taxpayers money to subsidise child care costs for all parents. The Department of Health is already spending £2 million in grant aid this year to support voluntary organisations to increase the amount of child care for under fives.

For children of school age the Department of Employment is spending £45 million over several years on schemes administered through Training and Enterprise Councils. In the first 9 months this initiative provided 2,300 more places for out-of-school child care with a further 2,000 places in development. The eventual target is 50,000 more places.

There has been a steady growth in both private and voluntary day nursery provision, for example between 1988 and 1992 the number of private day nurseries more than doubled from 1355 to 3400. In 1965/66 less than 130,000 children under the age of five attended day nurseries, play groups or were looked after by childminders. In 1991/92 the number had increased to almost 930,000. And in my own Department, as I have already mentioned, we are introducing help with child care costs for working families on low incomes.

Women as carers

Another important role for women is that of carer and we recognise the valuable role families play in providing care in the community. Over 60% of carers are women and they spend much of their lives helping friends and relatives to lead, as far as possible, full and independent lives in their own homes. Many carers are women of working age and although some are in employment, others are not and are having difficulty combining working with caring responsibilities. We appreciate that many carers have good reasons for wanting to continue in their jobs.

In March 1993 the Department of Health held a seminar attended by carers and employers, to discuss ways in which employers can help by adopting enlightened personnel policies, which need not impose a financial burden, such as use of flexible working patterns, job sharing, part-time working, special leave, career breaks etc. Much is to be gained on both sides – employers retain experienced staff, and enhanced employee commitment; carers gain status, respect and increased job satisfaction.

Increasingly Important Role Of Parents

The Government recognises the importance of ensuring that pupils understand the importance of good parenting, and are encouraged to develop the skills and attitudes that will enable them to manage their relationships in a responsible manner.

Schools are an important influence on our young people's behaviour. Education about personal relationships and parenthood can help today's children to acquire the knowledge, skills and attitudes they need to become tomorrow's confident and competent parents. Section 1 of the Education Reform Act 1988 requires that the curriculum as a whole for all maintained schools should prepare young people for the "opportunities, responsibilities and experiences of adult life". Adult relationships, marriage and parenthood are among those responsibilities.

Within National Curriculum science, pupils aged 11 to 14 are required to "understand the process of conception in human beings", to "know about physical and emotional changes that take place during adolescence"; and to learn about "the factors necessary for the well-being of young children in the early stages of their development". Pressure on curriculum time means that now is not the time for adding new subjects to the National Curriculum. The priority now is for stability. The Government will consider carefully responses to consultation on the proposals for a revised National Curriculum.

Under these proposals the mandatory curriculum for 5 to 14 year olds would be significantly streamlined, especially outside the core subjects of English, Mathematics and Science. The intention is to slim down what must be taught – not to add to it – in order to leave schools with an overall margin of roughly 20% of time to use at their own discretion.

The former National Curriculum Council advised that family life education should be a key component of schools' programmes of personal and social education. Non-statutory guidance on Health Education and Education for Citizenship, issued to all maintained schools in 1990, gave a significant place to consideration of the content of family life education and ways of integrating it into the curriculum.

Schools themselves can organise and manage the curriculum they deliver. Comprehensive programmes of personal and social education within the wider school curriculum help children to understand the importance of good parenting. Life skills training of this type can encourage them to develop the skills and attitudes to enable them to manage their relationships responsibly.

Conclusion

I hope this contribution has been helpful, and of interest. I realise there are many subjects on which I have not touched, and many that have probably been inadequately explored. I have, however, endeavoured to give not a straightforward Government statement, but a contribution to a discussion which, if the Year of the Family is to mean anything at all, must be wide ranging and involve everyone. The family is not a concept to be owned by Government, or political party, or any single institution. But the very fact of having a year so named at all, and the fact that so many can attend a conference like this, is evidence of attachment not simply to an idea or an institution, but something of real and lasting value, whatever its permutations might be. I suggest the common link in successful families, within or outside marriage, is the success of relationships, and the supplying of the security for the child that strong relationships engender. I sincerely hope that this recognition will be one of the good things to come from the International Year of the Family 1994.

3

FAMILIES AND THE FUTURE: A EUROPEAN PERSPECTIVE

Robin Guthrie

I intend firstly to address the nature of the European Institutions and their relationships to each other. It does help to understand how the Council of Europe, the European Union and other international organisations can help or hinder in the development of family policies and policies for children. I will try to put the European Union and the Council of Europe into context. I then have a prepared text which I will use as the basis of my presentation of what the Council of Europe is actually doing at the moment.

Council Of Europe

The Council of Europe was founded in 1949 by 10 member states, on the basis of clear, simple and very recognisable principles: human rights, the rule of law (that is to say essentially an independent judiciary) and pluralist democracy (that is to say basically the right of any citizen to form a political party).

It was founded moreover with the aim of achieving greater unity amongst its members for the purpose of safeguarding and realising these ideals and principles, and to facilitate the economic and social progress of the member states. The methods of work, also prescribed in the first article of the Statute, are specifically "discussion, agreements and common action".

I sometimes hear politicians who have reservations about how things are going in the Europe of the Twelve describing the Europe of independent, co-operating states they would like to see. I have to say to them "Minister, you have just described the Council of Europe"! But it is not, unfortunately, generally recognised that the institution already exists. That lack of recognition is one of the weaknesses of European development today. The Council of Europe is essentially an instrument of inter-governmental co-operation, not of central decision-making. That is why it is overshadowed by the organs of the European Union where real power and real money do reside.

The organs of the Council of Europe are two: the Parliamentary Assembly and the Committee of Ministers of Foreign Affairs of the member states. The Parliamentary Assembly is made up of members of national parliaments, people who have already been elected to their national parliament, who are then nominated by their parliament to serve also in Strasbourg. They are therefore very different from the members of the European Parliament, who are directly elected and who also meet in Strasbourg. The Parliamentary Assembly, has no legislative powers and cannot instruct the Committee of Ministers what to do. It has considerable political influence, but ultimately only the Committee of Ministers can decide what the Council of Europe will actually do.

It is perhaps a weakness of the Council of Europe that it is the governments, in the Committee of Ministers, that take all the decisions. In the European Union there is a balance between the major institutions, which the Council of Europe does not enjoy. That does affect the work that we are able to do in all areas including those of family policy where governments are sometimes not very adventurous in what they are willing to agree to, what they are willing to sign up to, whereas free-ranging politicians from parliaments can be more imaginative. But the Parliamentary Assembly does have an important role in debating issues, in clarifying political priorities, albeit without the power to compel the governments to do as they might wish. It also has a power of initiating ideas, of applying pressure and thereby of helping the Committee of Ministers, and through them the governments, to develop their policies.

As the prime guardian of human rights and instrument of inter-governmental co-operation between nations, the Council of Europe straddles the Continent. In 1949 there were 10 members; by 1989 there were 24. The political changes in 1989 found the Council of Europe more than any other organisation ready for the expansion of Europe into a single instead of a divided continent. Since 1989 eight new members have joined, and more are about to. There is a profound difference between the relationship of these new democracies with Strasbourg and their relationship with Brussels. They come to Strasbourg as democratic equals. It is indeed very exciting to see each country arrive in Strasbourg at first with associate status and subsequently in full membership, as democratic equals in the Council of Europe. They go to Brussels as beggars, drawn by the power and money that rest there in contrast to the ideals and principles on which Strasbourg is founded. Nevertheless Poland, Hungary, the Czech Republic, Slovakia, Slovenia, Romania, Bulgaria, Latvia and Estonia are now full members of the Council of Europe and others have applied, including Lithuania to make up the Baltic States, Albania, the Ukraine, and Russia. When Russia joins the Council of Europe that will be a very significant threshold and will change the Organisation in ways which we cannot yet fully appreciate.

Our first tasks in Central and Eastern Europe lay in the fields of human rights, the rule of law and pluralist democracy, helping the new democracies to establish democratic institutions and providing technical assistance. It is the characteristic of the Council of Europe to be concerned first of all with human rights and that is perhaps the most distinguishing factor to people outside it. But it is also recognised that you cannot have successful democratic institutions if you do not also have successful social and economic policies. Our technical assistance has accordingly been as much at the level of, for example, social policy, social security, health policy and the like as it has been concerned with democratic institution building. Ralf Dahrendorf distinguished between the *politiques constitutionelles* of democratic institution – building at a time of radical change and the *politiques quotidiennes* of daily life, recognising that however exciting and challenging were the politics of revolutionary change they would fail if the *politiques quotidiennes* – the politics of everyday life – were not equally successful.

These have indeed, for the whole continent, been massive changes. The Central and Eastern European countries have been facing wholly new challenges but the Western European countries are facing similar challenges, if in a different form. For example, there is not a single country in the continent that is not radically reviewing the form, the nature and the content of its health services. One thing here does worry me: the extent and force of the ideological thrusts from the West. A western institution will go into a new democracy determined to organise the social security system on a free-market basis with private insurance, to a degree not prevalent even in the West. At the receiving end people will say "Well that is actually a bit difficult to attach to our history, it is difficult to latch on to our institutions – this is where we are, this is where we start", to which the response has been, as often as not, "If you can't take our medicine then you can't have our help". "What was so undemocratic about the social security systems in eastern Europe before 1989?", an American colleague asked me. It could be argued that they were more "democratic", if that is the right criterion, than the western social security systems have by and large been. But that is not the only criterion by which one judges a social security system. What one does need to understand, particularly with a social security system, is the nature of it, its present form and, above all, its history. Despite the uniformity which was imposed on eastern Europe in the totalitarian era, all the social security systems have a different history, have a different form and require a slightly different approach to development in the new circumstances. Since we are all facing significant changes, and we are all looking for solutions to the same problems but from different starting points, the solutions that are found in eastern Europe may have as many lessons for us in the West as the solutions we have found in the last 40 years are likely to have for the East.

European Union

So much for the Council of Europe. The European Union had very different origins. The crucial development was the creation of the Coal and Steel community. My impression of that post-war period in European affairs is that it was a bit like the primeval swamp. There was a certain fluidity in the situation; you could not tell what kind of microbes were going to get together, what kind of amoebas were going to form and what kind of monsters would then arise. People were searching for almost any solution, so long as it would work and so long as it would meet certain fundamental criteria. None of the ideal solutions that were put forward at that time came into effect. People were working with an ideal in sight but with a very pragmatic approach to what opportunities were available. The Coal and Steel community was crucial because if France and Germany shared a steel industry they couldn't fight each other, it would just be nonsense to be making tanks in opposition to each other in the same factories. From that point the various European communities developed essentially on a basis of economic goals and common economic interests. It was clear in the debate in the European Parliament earlier this year on the progress of the negotiations of the accession of the four new states to the Community that what was being defended by the Twelve was the economic *acquis* of the Community rather than any ideals and principles which might be associated with a pan-European vision. This does make a practical difference.

One tiny illustration: the European Pharmacopoeia, for which I am responsible. The Council of Europe sees it essentially in the context of human rights as an instrument of consumer protection, to ensure that the individual may have some protection over the kind of medicaments that he or she may buy or be prescribed. The European Union has now signed the Convention of the European Pharmacopoeia and become a full member in its own right, alongside the twelve member states who already belonged individually. At once a different perspective emerges of the basic purpose of the European Pharmacopoeia as a vehicle for ensuring the free market in pharmaceutical goods, and the free operation of pharmaceutical companies across the continent: a radically different concept of the purpose of one and the same institution. These two concepts are not necessarily incompatible, but one must not be allowed to obliterate the other.

One of the great strengths of the European Union and one of the things that I think holds great promise for the future is its institutional structure with the Council of Ministers on the one hand, meeting often with specialist ministers, and representing the interests of governments; the Parliament, independent of the Council of Ministers, often fighting it openly and publicly; and the Commission, with its own independent capacity to act, reporting to the Council of Ministers and to the Parliament.

Whatever adjustments need to be made to the powers of these bodies – and adjustments are needed – this seems to me to be a strong institutional structure for future development and for political debate.

Social Policy And The Family

Cooperation between the European Union and the Council of Europe varies according to subject matter. In social policy it can be quite difficult to engage in co-operation or even in debate with the European Union because of the different starting points of the two organisations. For the Union, social policy has again an economic origin. The Green Paper on Social Policy was a very useful document indeed bringing together a great deal of information, setting it in a framework and debating the issues and priorities. It has now been succeeded by the White Paper. But there is nothing about the family or the importance of the family or the support of the family as such. There cannot be because it is not in the Union's mandate. What we do find are references to reconciling employment and family life, to equality between women and men especially at work, and to various other aspects of family life in relation to employment and working life. That is not to decry the importance of this document at all, but simply to illustrate the difference between the approach of the Council of Europe and of the European Union.

In the Council of Europe the intergovernmental co-operation to which I have referred takes place under the authority of the Committee of Ministers by means of steering committees. The mechanisms are important. At some point on any particular issue you have got to get everybody together in one room talking to each other (via interpreters). That is how "discussion, agreements and common action" can be developed on each of the topics with which the Council is concerned. It is sometimes, as you can imagine, a rather tedious means: meetings of two or three days or more with 40–50 people, some of whom know what they are talking about, some of whom will not speak at all, some of whom know how to manipulate the machine to achieve their objectives and some of whom are tactically relatively inept, trying to engage in debate and discussion about very important technical issues. But it is effective. Supporting the steering committees, composed of government specialists, we have the secretariat which sometimes has a certain professional capacity as well, and expert consultants from outside to prepare reports. That is an economic and effective way of working in terms of producing some quite interesting and important material with the minimum of resources.

So far as the family is concerned, the European Social Policy Committee, which is our Steering Committee on Social Policy, has broad terms of reference. I will quote from them because they do reflect the breadth of the work that the Council of Europe is able to undertake. First, "to examine current social issues in Europe, including family policies, child welfare, and the situation of the elderly, with a view to identifying common trends and promoting effective practices" – a sharing in other words of concerns between governments. Secondly, "to address social problems in Europe, particularly as they affect families, children, the elderly and the marginalised and specifically problems arising from poverty and social exclusion, with a view to making proposals for meeting these challenges at the European level". The terms of reference go on to include the exchange of information on developments and experiences in different countries, the need to follow up the conclusions and recommendations of the Conference of European Ministers for Family Affairs, and the power to co-operate with other institutions.

Those terms of reference are broad enough. But besides the European Social Policy Committee we have a number of other activities and elements which impinge on the well-being of families. Supported by the Directorate of Legal Affairs is a Committee of Experts working on family law, working at the present time to develop a European Convention on the exercise by children of their rights which will match the UN Convention on the Rights of the Child, not by repeating it but by spelling out the means of implementing the United Nations Convention in Europe. It seems to us that the United Nations Convention says most of what is needed but what has to happen beyond that is some kind of agreement between states on how they will actually make it effective. My colleagues in Education of course have a considerable influence on the policies for children. Housing is dealt with by my colleagues in the Directorate of Environment and Local Authorities. In other areas for which I am responsible we have the European Population Committee, the European Employment Committee and the European Social Security Committee – they are all of them intergovernmental steering committees – and we have also the initiatives and concern of the Parliamentary Assembly and of the Local Authority politicians in the Congress of Local and Regional Authorities.

It is the European Social Policy Committee that is the focus for all this activity in respect of the family. We have identified four challenges faced by families which we think are of particular importance. The first is the political, the economic and the social changes in society which have affected and will affect the family as an institution. The second is the fact that the family takes on different forms from one country to another and even also within the same country. This is a dynamic process which is creating new forms of families and different family-life cycles in a way which previous generations have not experienced. The third challenge for a family is how to bring to bear on its own needs all the resources that society in theory is making available for it. The problem is one of co-ordination between the different social policies and the different departments and agencies involved. The fourth challenge lies in the dramatic changes that are taking place in family structures, throughout the continent.

These challenges call for the adoption of coherent and integrated family policies. It will continue to be necessary to accord adequate protection and support to families in order that they can take on their functions within society. The potential of every family must be promoted, in particular those of the poorest families, to encourage their independence and their capacity to fulfil their responsibilities whilst family members retain the self-respect essential to every human being. The problem is to get these principles into the practices of governments and indeed of individuals throughout the Continent.

Council Of Europe And Family Policy

In pursuit of that objective, to try to make some of these ideals and ideas effective, the Council of Europe has undertaken four main activities, and I will just speak briefly on each. The first is a Recommendation on Coherent and Integrated Family Policies. The second concerns the Conference for Ministers responsible for Family Affairs. The third is specifically concerned with Childhood Policies; and the fourth is a series of Intergovernmental Studies and Research which are concentrated on particular issues.

The first therefore is the Recommendation on Coherent and Integrated Family Policies. I mentioned that the Council of Europe proceeds by discussion, agreements and common action. Agreements take the form sometimes of conventions, sometimes of protocols, sometimes of Recommendations (with a capital 'R'). Recommendations and Conventions are form of treaty. They have a legal basis. Once adopted by the nations of Europe, through the Committee of Ministers at the Council of Europe, they can have some influence on national policies, and indeed not just influence on national policies but support for national policies. Whereas national policies are decided in the capitals of the member states, our purpose in the Council is to inform those policies by the sharing of experience and the development of ideas in the common forum of the Council of Europe, so that national policies can be improved and developed. Nearly all countries have some kind of a family policy, more or less coherent, generally based on legislation concerning the family, on income transfers, and on services directed specifically to the family. What we are trying to do is to advocate measures which will be in line with the needs and expectations of families. These are themselves constantly changing. They focus on how families can realise their own plans, particularly in matters such as housing and education. In this context we would emphasise the significance of preventive family policy, and the scope for guidance, counselling and services at different stages of development for each family, to reduce vulnerability.

In all European countries it has been the family where interaction between generations has happened and where personal relationships have developed. Parents themselves are responsible for bringing up their children according to the basic values of democratic society. We therefore give high priority to educational and to mediation services which facilitate the resolution of family conflicts. But as Alistair Burt made clear earlier in this book, to achieve a coherent and integrated family policy is not easy. Any such policy crosses existing administrative boundaries and has in effect to be the co-ordinating factor between the different sectors of government that affect the family. That is a trick that few governments can claim to have pulled off completely. The intention behind the Recommendation to which I referred is to clarify what such a policy entails and so to help the decision makers in the capitals of the member states to accommodate their own national laws and practices closer to the ideal. That Recommendation is in preparation and I hope will be published by the end of the year.

The second activity I mentioned is the Conference of European Ministers responsible for Family Affairs. This has its own history and something of a life of its own. In 1959, during the Congress of the International Union of Family Organisations, there was a spontaneous informal meeting between Ministers of seven countries with responsibility for Family Affairs. They decided that it would be sensible for them and their colleagues to get together. Since 1969 the Council of Europe has provided the secretariat for the conferences which are held every two years. The 1987 Conference was on "Recent Developments in Family Structures and Future Perspectives". That gave rise to a project which we, in the Council of Europe, completed in 1991 on the problems associated with recent changes in family structures. The report is available. The 1989 Conference concentrated on methods of child upbringing in Europe and the role of family services, and that led to the Project on Childhood Policies which I will be referring to in a moment. That in turn was reinforced by the 1993 Conference on "Family Policies, Children's Rights, and Parental Responsibilities". The next one, the 24th – it is one of the longest standing European Conferences at Ministerial level – will be in Helsinki in June next year and will be on the status and role of the father, with implications for family policies.

The Project on Childhood Policies is an ambitious project which incorporates no fewer than 12 of the steering committees within the Council of Europe. The different interests within the Council of Europe concerned with the family and the difficulty of co-ordinating them reflect exactly the kind of difficulties that each government has in bringing coherence to the different perspectives on family policy within governments. The recent United Nations Convention on the Rights of the Child has given new impetus to that particular task. There is intense discussion on the delicate matter of the extent to which children should be granted individual rights *vis-à-vis* family and society. But we have learnt much in recent years about the importance of ensuring those rights: they cannot be assumed. Probably if we look more deeply back into history we will find this not to be a new phenomenon, but the opportunity to redress the balance is new.

The situation of children in European societies is itself changing. Birth-rates in Europe are declining, sometimes below the rate of reproducing the population, and yet the costs of bringing up children to individual households and of providing them with health care and social protection to the nation as a whole remain considerable. It must be said that for most countries in membership of the Council of Europe, the vision of our children's future reflected in the social and economic arrangements for them do not reflect a coherent pattern but rather consist of an accumulation of often incoherent measures. The concomitant of the lower birth rate, together with other factors, is that the population of Europe is ageing, and the proportion of social expenditure devoted to the elderly population is increasing.

It is in the context of those developments that we need to ask ourselves the question: "Where do we stand as a society in relation to our children?". Considering the economic and budgetary constraints that governments and everybody are facing at the moment, that becomes an urgent question. For a long time children have not been given rights of their own but considered in the context of other policy fields, whether family or health or crime or social security or whatever. But the United Nations Convention has opened the way to a new approach. It is that challenge that the Project on Childhood Policies is trying to take up, developing mechanisms and programmes for the implementation of the Convention. Beyond that we are trying to provide an overall response to the challenges faced by children in today's society and tomorrow's: challenges social, economic, demographic and cultural. Our aim is to develop fundamental principles for a coherent policy for children: we even talk of a European Childhood Policy. The topic areas are: the repercussions on children of political, social and cultural changes in our societies; the importance for children of the family environment for development and well-being; the effect of changes in family structures and the need for increasing social responsibility for children, including services such as consultation centres for parents and children, child day-care services, and arrangements to facilitate the reconciliation of family and working life; and fourthly, the relationship between family policies on the one hand and childhood policies on the other, particularly as children themselves grow and mature into independent citizens. One thinks, for example, of the great difficulties for children who have been in care when suddenly they are no longer in care, one of the crucial issues which is not I think anywhere fully treated.

The Childhood Policies Project began in 1992 and will last four years. An open Conference in Spain in December 1994 focused on "The Evolution of the Role of Children in Family Life: Participation and Negotiation". That practical working conference should lead to recommendations which will affect our work and the work of governments. So that is the Childhood Policies Project, a major effort therefore by governments within the Council of Europe to implicate the work at international level and thus to help national governments.

The fourth area to which I wanted to refer is that of the specific studies that we carry out through what is called a Co-ordinated Research Programme. That is initiated every year and each one lasts for two years, so we have usually three going on at any one time. The European Social Policy Committee determines the topic and then recommends individual specialists to take part from among those nominated by the member states. In 1993, for example, work was completed by a study group on "street children". The report, and also the national reports on which the final report drew, are fascinating reading. A second study group has completed researching the issue of "the interaction between the providers of family services" in member states. The final report will be published shortly and it is obviously a very important subject.

These then are the main activities of the Council of Europe in this area. In concluding, perhaps I could just summarise briefly the attitude that the Council of Europe takes in these matters and the key principles which we think could underlie European policies for families at this stage in our development. Some of this, you will say, is so obvious it does not need saying, but on the other hand if you do not say, it cannot be taken for granted. There are five principles. First, that public authorities should ensure that a framework exists which favours the well-being and autonomy of families, with appropriate day-care, medical, social, educational and cultural services. Secondly, the plurality of family structures must be recognised and their specific needs acknowledged: families based on marriage, families based on cohabitation, single parent families, broken families, step families, multiple families, and so on. Thirdly, the family should be the place where the rights of the different members are equally taken into account.

The question of equality between women and men which also relates to employment practices is one of the most important developments in this field. An interesting thing about the World Population Conference in Cairo which I attended, contributing the European point of view, was the emphasis on women. That is, not just a matter of equality between women and men (which is a matter of particular concern to the Council of Europe in the context of human rights); not just a question of human dignity; not just a recognition of the value of every individual; not just a question of the education of women in the developing world as being the best means of contraception; but actually an acknowledgement at this stage in the development of the human race, if we are to meet the challenges which the Cairo Conference amongst others was posing, that what we need perhaps is less of the masculine qualities of the human psyche which have dominated the development of the human race until now, and more of the feminine qualities of the human psyche, which are by no means exclusive to women. This emphasis on the role of women in society is therefore something which goes very deep indeed and places in an interesting context the question of redefining and strengthening the role of the father in the family. Fourthly, it is important to recognise that governments have a particular responsibility to protect families in periods of economic crisis, and to take preventive measures to reduce the number of families living in poverty. And fifthly, families should be able to participate in community life, not to be isolated but to be part of the mainstream of community life and decision-making, and indeed of political influence.

The role of the public authorities, which is our particular concern in the Council of Europe, is then to create the circumstances for the establishment of a family unit in which the individual can develop in safety, solidarity, self-respect and with respect for fundamental rights, on the basis of legal, social, cultural and economic criteria, and taking account of the special needs of the different types of families and the different stages of family life. It is perhaps one of the most significant challenges facing our society today. I hope that we in the Council of Europe can help the nations of Europe to meet it.

4

IMPLICATIONS OF CHANGES IN FAMILY STRUCTURE FOR THE LAW

Kathleen Marshall

S COTTISH legal and social work activists are still working their
way through proposals for changes in family law.

Each of the three key sets of proposals to which I shall be referring
grounds its recommendations in perceived changes in family structure.

The White Paper *Scotland's Children: Proposals for Child Care Policy
and Law*, published in August 1993, proclaims, in its Foreword by the
Secretary of State, that "The law is an essential expression of society's
values".

The Paper acknowledges (para.1.3) that "Family structure is
changing". It points to the increase in the proportion of children born
outwith marriage, and lists a number of the changes which have taken place;
the drop in the marriage rate, the increase in the divorce rate, the significant
increase in the number of children living in one – parent families, the
increasing involvement of women in all areas of life, and the consequent
changing domestic role of men, the increased dependency of young adults
taking advantage of higher education, and the need to take account, in
family policy and law, of the variety of forms of family life co-existing in the
newly emerging multi-cultural Scotland.

Although the structure of the family has changed, it is still seen as the
sacrosanct, basic building block of society. It is still valued, and the changes
in the law proposed by the White Paper are meant to be an expression of
that value. "Despite these changes," the Paper says (para. 1.10), "families
remain and will remain the foundation of care for children and the
development of young people."

The Scottish Law Commission's *Report on Family Law* of May 1992
also grapples with the implications for the law of the changes in family
structure referred to above. The increase in cohabitation, no longer restrain
ed by the stigma of "living in sin", poses many legal dilemmas in relation to
the cohabitants themselves and their children. The increasing value placed
internationally on the rights of children has led the Commission to ponder
on how these values could best be expressed in the law of Scotland.

A Scottish Office Consultation Document – *The Future of Adoption Law in Scotland*, issued in June, 1993, also deals with the implications of changes in family structure. Chapter 1 of the Paper states that:

"It is generally accepted that the purpose of adoption is to secure a child in a permanent substitute family with new parents where the birth parents are either unwilling or unable to care for him."

The apparent disintegration of the married parent family lasting a childhood has posed particular questions for the adoption process, rooted, I would suggest in the uncomfortable awareness that adoption law may be trying to legislate for a permanence and stability that can no longer be guaranteed in the real world.

In this chapter I intend:

- to explain and explore the response of the law to changes in family structure as set out in these three documents
- to look at what tensions remain unresolved
- to touch on the issue of the relationship of the law to social change. Is the law a tool for change, or is it a mirror reflecting change? To what extent is it legitimate to use the law as a means of engineering social change, or, what seems more likely today, to set up a bulwark against the direction of change in which society is drifting? Is the law indeed, as the White Paper on Child Care Law proclaims, "an essential expression of society's values"? Or does the law itself seek to circumscribe the sacrosanct?

The UN Convention On The Rights Of The Child

Before embarking upon a consideration of the current proposals for law reform, it is necessary to take into account the influence of the United Nations Convention on the Rights of the Child.

Although not an integral part of UK law, ratification of the Convention by the UK Government in December 1991 committed it to bringing the law, policy and practice of the UK into line with the standards set by the Convention.

The Convention makes clear and radical statements about the rights of children to:

protection from neglect, abuse and exploitation
provision of services to promote their development, and
participation in decisions which affect them.

The Convention is not, however, a charter for rampant youth liberty and individualism. The Preamble declares its authors to be:

"Convinced that the family, as the fundamental group of society and the natural environment for the growth and well-being of all its members and particularly of children, should be afforded the necessary protection and assistance so that it can fully assume its responsibilities within the community."

Article 5 of the Convention emphasises the role of the family, and the responsibility of parents in particular:

"to provide, in a manner consistent with the evolving capacities of the child, appropriate direction and guidance in the exercise by the child of the rights recognised in the present Convention."

Article 18 of the Convention obliges States Parties to,

"render appropriate assistance to parents and legal guardians in the performance of their child-rearing responsibilities"

and to,

"ensure the development of institutions, facilities and services for the care of children".

Particular emphasis is laid on the need to ensure the provision of child care services for the children of working parents.

Child Care Law Reform – The White Paper

The White Paper, *Scotland's Children: Proposals for Child Care Policy and Law*, starts with a statement of basic principles based on the UN Convention. At several points in the Paper, emphasis is laid on the importance of supporting families as the basic unit of society, and the related child care policy of supporting children within their families wherever possible rather than removing them into state care. We are talking here of families in respect of which there is some concern about the welfare of the children.

There is a rather woolly reference to the possibility of a wider use of respite care. Historically seen more as a resource for families with children with special needs, the White Paper acknowledges (para.3.15) that,

"it can have a more widespread application. It can allow the child's usual carers to continue willingly in that role, where the absence of support might precipitate breakdown of the arrangements."

There is an acknowledgement here that the pressures (and perhaps also the values – although that is not referred to) of today's society are more likely to culminate in a breakdown in the family unit than they were in days gone by. Both policy and fiscal concern would seem to point to family support as being a valuable option.

Day care is also put forward as an important plank in the family support policy. As well as (para.3.14),

"offering parents greater opportunities to meet personal and social needs. Day care also fulfils an important preventive role by providing a range of resources from mutual self-help to parent-craft training and health education. This short or medium term intervention can serve in many instances to prevent the need for statutory intervention or reception into care at a later stage."

If we look again at the list of changes in family structure referred to above, it is clear that families as entities are vulnerable today in a way that they never were before. They need a lot more support, and, if they are truly valued, that must mean a lot more valuable support – more resources.

At the risk of sounding fanciful and straying outwith my professional expertise, I would like to explain to you the shift I perceive in organisational units at the present time; a shift at the individual and family level which is reflected to some extent in the political world.

Politically, we are witnessing the emergence in Europe of small nation states, under the shadow of a larger European Union. It is as if the emergence of the larger body has created a framework on a scale which permits the smaller units to re-emerge, and seems almost to hark back to the ancient structure of the Holy Roman Empire embracing smaller principalities.

In the family sphere, the breakdown of the clan/tribe/extended family into the nuclear family and now into individualism, has required a corresponding development of an over-arching structure – the State – to sustain it, viz.;

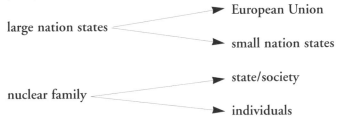

I will take up later issues relating to attempts by the State to engineer or stop the course of social change through legislation. The point I wish to make just now is that, no matter whether we decry the demise of the family, or whether we see it as not having disappeared but just changed, we have to acknowledge that families are a lot more individualistic than they used to be.

The White Paper itself refers to parents meeting "personal and social needs".

The State has provided women with some options to remaining in abusive and oppressive relationships.

The State has enacted measures to protect children from abuse or neglect within the family.

There has been increasing recognition of the rights of individuals to protection and development. By facilitating that protection and development, the State has dug the first turf in the process of undermining the family as previously constituted. If it nevertheless values the family, and wishes to encourage and facilitate its survival, it must earnestly provide the resources, including family education, that will help achieve this end.

Family support, respite care and day care are all good ideas, but tokenism will not be enough. If there are to be families in the future, the initial investment must take place now.

The move towards individualism

The move towards individualism is also reflected in the status of children. The increase in recognition of child abuse within the family, the acknowledgement of the right of children as individuals to be protected from it, and the increasing rate of domestic breakdown, have contributed to a situation in which it is no longer tenable to define children in terms of their relationship with particular adults or stable family groups. Of course most children are still, thankfully, not abused, nor exploited, and are securely cared for, but the legal system, in its acknowledgement of the rights and status of children, has had to take account of the significant levels of abuse and insecurity which do exist; has had to concede that there may be situations in which the interests of parent and child diverge, and to make provision for this.

The authors of the White Paper have clearly struggled with identifying the optimum point of balance between respect for the responsibilities and rights of parents and the needs and rights of children who may require protection.

Current Scottish law on the protection of children was drafted before the exposure of the extent and depth of child abuse within the family. During the life of the Social Work (Scotland) Act 1968, some amendments have been made, notably the introduction of the 'Safeguarder', an independent person to represent the interests of the child where these appear to conflict with those of the parent. This followed the tragic death in England of Maria Colwell, which highlighted the difficulties encountered by social workers in trying to address conflicting interests.

The measure was introduced late into Scotland, and half-heartedly applied. It has however become a significant focus for reform, having been referred to with approval by Lord Clyde in his 1992 *Report of the Inquiry into the Removal of Children from Orkney in February 1991* (Chapter 17 and Recs. 80–84). The White Paper subsequently stated (para.6.19 and 6.20) that:

"The Government have decided to emphasise the current powers of hearings and sheriffs, as soon as cases come before them, to consider appointment of Safeguarders in order to ensure that they play an active part in the proceedings... The development of the Safeguarder's role and functions is seen as providing added benefits for children who come to children's hearings and courts. The Secretary of State has therefore set in hand a review of the existing role and functions of Safeguarders."

The Scottish Law Commission's Report On Family Law

A new emphasis on children as individuals with their own rights and interests is also apparent in the Scottish Law Commission's *Report on Family Law,* May 1992. In common with the White Paper on child care law, this document is peppered with references to the UN Convention on the Rights of the Child, and often takes its cue from it.

It places a lot of emphasis on parental responsibility, by, for example, setting out a proposed statutory statement of what it entails (Rec. 1,(b)):

"It should be provided that a parent has in relation to his or her child a responsibility, so far as is practicable and in the interests of the child,

(i) to safeguard and promote the child's health, development and welfare

(ii) to provide, in a manner appropriate to the child's stage of development, direction and guidance to the child

(iii) if not living with the child, to maintain personal relations and direct contact with the child on a regular basis

(iv) to act as the child's legal representative and, in that capacity, to administer, in the interests of the child, any property belonging to the child."

These responsibilities are to be in addition to other specific statutory responsibilities.

The statement of responsibilities is complemented by an ascription of rights regarded as necessary to enable parents to fulfil their responsibilities (Rec. 4):

"In addition to any rights conferred by any other enactment a parent should have the right, so long as the child is under the age of 16,

(a) to have the child living with him or her, or otherwise to regulate the child's residence

(b) to control, direct or guide, in a manner appropriate to the child's stage of development, the child's upbringing

(c) if not living with the child, to maintain personal relations and direct contact with the child

(d) to act as the child's legal representative and, in that capacity to administer the child's property, and to act, or give consent, on behalf of the child in any transaction having legal effect where the child is incapable of acting or consenting on his or her own behalf."

Recommendation 88 of the Report proposes to abolish the remnants of the legal status of illegitimacy, whilst Recommendation 5 proposes awarding parental rights automatically to unmarried fathers who currently have to go to court to obtain them.

Problems in relation to unmarried fathers have become particularly acute with the rise in extra-marital cohabitation, and the increasing instability of relationships – marital or non-marital. The Commission's Report stated (para 2.48):

"Given that about 25% of all children born in Scotland in recent years have been born out of wedlock, and that the number of couples cohabiting outside marriage is now substantial, it seems to us that the balance has now swung in favour of the view that parents are parents, whether married to each other or not."

This issue will be developed further under the heading of Cohabitation.

The conclusion from this part of the discussion is that the response to the changing face of the family has been, not to give up on it, but to clarify responsibilities and rights and to neutralise some of the legal disadvantages, for fathers and children, of births out of wedlock.

The individualisation of the child is recognised in a number of proposals, e.g.,

"10.(a) It should be provided that any person taking any major decision relating to a child in the exercise of any parental responsibility or right should, whenever practicable, ascertain the views of the child regarding the decision and give due consideration to them, having regard to the child's age and maturity.

(b) for this purpose there should be a presumption that a child of the age of 12 or more has sufficient maturity to express a reasonable view regarding the decision, but this should not carry any implication that the views of a child under that age are not worthy of consideration."

This principle of participation in decision making is in line with Article 12 of the UN Convention on the Rights of the Child, and is carried through into the court sphere by other recommendations:

"31. For the avoidance of any doubt it should be made clear that the child concerned may apply for an order relating to parental responsibilities or rights, guardianship or the administration of his or her property...

34(a). Rules of court should ensure that a child who is capable of forming his or her own views and who wishes to have his or her views put directly before a court in any proceedings relating to parental responsibilities or rights, or guardianship or the administration of the child's property, has a readily available procedural mechanism for doing so."

Cohabitation

Reference has already been made to the increase in recent years of cohabitation as opposed to marriage, and the consequent proposal to amend the law to remove the legal disadvantages suffered by fathers and children in this situation.

The basic premise on which the Scottish Law Commission proceeds is that cohabitants freely choose to avoid the legal consequences of marriage. It would therefore be inappropriate to approximate the laws of cohabitation too closely to those of marriage. It would also be difficult, because there is often no clear point at which a legal partnership or commitment can be said to begin.

Consideration was, for example, given (para.16.15) to a,

"comprehensive system of financial provision on termination of a cohabitation comparable to the system of financial provision on divorce in the Family Law (Scotland) Act 1985."

The Commission decided against such comprehensive provision on the grounds that:

"That would be to impose a regime of property sharing, and in some cases continuing financial support, on couples who may well have opted for cohabitation in order to avoid such consequences."

The Commission decided instead in favour of a more modest provision aimed at redressing some of the unfairness that could arise through lack of any provision.

There is a problem for the law here in that, in theory, everyone is presumed to know the law. "Ignorance of the law excuses no man", as the ancient saying expresses it. The reality, as we all know, is somewhat different. To many, the institution of marriage has come to be seen as unduly restrictive and unnecessary. "Why should we need a piece of paper to cement our relationship?" they ask.

How much thought does the average person really give to the actual legal consequences of marriage, and the legal implications of not being married? I have personally, for example, spoken with many unmarried fathers who were completely unaware of their vulnerable legal status; that they had no rights of custody or guardianship over their children; that they were not, for example, entitled to give consent to their child's medical treatment.

How many people, opting for cohabitation instead of marriage, have really thought through the implications in terms of mutual financial support, upbringing of children, pensions, insurance, or termination of the relationship by separation or death?

The Scottish Law Commission did consider this. A public consultation on the subject of cohabitation had, they said (para.16.1),

> "...confirmed us in our view that there is a strong case for some limited reform of Scottish private law to enable certain legal difficulties faced by cohabiting couples to be overcome and to enable certain anomalies to be remedied. However we are also confirmed in our impression that this is a subject on which widely differing views are held. There is, in particular, a respectable view that it would be unwise to impose marriage like consequences on couples who have deliberately chosen not to marry. It was argued by some of those who commented on the discussion paper that the best approach would be to leave those who opt out of marriage to make their own legal arrangements by means, e.g., of cohabitation contracts, insurance policies and wills. Although we have considerable sympathy with this view, we doubt whether it is realistic to expect all cohabiting couples to make adequate private legal arrangements."

So the approach has been to reflect the changes in family structure by acknowledging the desire on the part of some to have unregulated relationships, but to ensure that extremes of harshness and unfairness arising out of this can be redressed. So far as children are concerned, the proposed heightened status of the unmarried father is seen primarily as an award of responsibilities rather than rights, and a recognition of the rights of the child to contact and support.

"Free love", the emotional battle-cry of the Sixties, has been shown to be a naïve concept. Relationships inevitably involve responsibility. Even if partners enter them blindly, the law must be vigilant to protect them against the consequences of their own blind optimism, especially where there is a power or resource imbalance, or children are born of the relationship.

The Adoption Law Review

The changes in family structure referred to earlier clearly have a relevance for the subject of adoption. The increase in cohabitation and extra-marital births has resulted in a greater social acceptance and less pressure on unmarried mothers to give their babies up for adoption – thus all but drying up the supply.

The Consultation Paper on The Future of Adoption Law in Scotland quotes (at para 1.2) the 1990 Third Quinquennial Report to Parliament under the Children Act 1975 to the effect that:

"Since 1982 there has been a shift in the age distribution of children involved in adoption applications, with very young children tending to form a smaller proportion of the total than in previous years and older children, particularly the 5–11 age group, accounting for a correspondingly higher share. The average age of children involved in applications has risen from 5.4 years in 1982 to 6.5 years in 1989."

There is considerable debate about whether adoption, as traditionally perceived, is appropriate for older children, who will have memories of previous attachments – good and bad – and who may well derive benefit from continuing contact of some description with some members of the birth family. The legal fiction that all ties with the birth family are relinquished and vested in the new family simply will not do.

There has been some debate about legal alternatives to adoption, e.g., using legal custody or the Scottish Law Commission's proposed new concept of guardianship to ensure *de facto* security for the child, without tampering with the child's legal identity.

There have also been proposals to introduce new forms of adoption which would allow it to co-exist with a degree of contact between the child and his or her birth family. The Consultation Paper acknowledges (para.7.18) the appropriateness in some cases of maintaining contact, but questions whether this should be in the context of adoption, or of some other category of permanent care. The Consultation Paper envisages (para.7.14) the court being able,

"to make an order relating to any other parental rights at the same time as the making of the adoption order."

This, however, should not be allowed to obscure the main purpose of the adoption, which involves (para.7.18) the,

"permanent placement of a child with alternative parents as though the child were born of the marriage."

As well as changes in the character of the adoption "supply", i.e., the children available for adoption, there has been a change in the "demand", the pool of those wishing to adopt.

There are more examples of cohabitation than there used to be. Should unmarried couples be allowed to adopt?

There is greater acceptance of homosexual relationships. Should gay men and lesbians be allowed to adopt?

There are more step-families. Should adoption of step-children be encouraged, discouraged, or subject to special arrangements?

In considering the position of unmarried couples, who are at present unable to adopt, The Review stated that:

"The changing nature of family structures was recognised, and it was suggested that the stability of the relationship was perhaps the most important factor to be taken into account. Reaction by respondents to this suggestion was mixed, but the balance of opinion seemed to favour relaxing the prohibition, even though it would contravene Article 6(1) of the European Convention on the Adoption of Children which prohibits adoption by unmarried couples. The absence of a legal relationship between the unmarried couple was, however, seen as a potential problem by both supporters and opponents of reform in the event of a separation taking place."

The Review group considered the proposals of the Scottish Law Commission referred to above, which would provide for some legal regulation of cohabitation. The group felt that implementation of the Commission's proposals would pave the way for removal of the prohibition on unmarried couples adopting. However it concluded that, until that happened (para2.6),

"it is proposed that the complete prohibition on joint adoption by a man and woman who are not married should remain."

Assuming that adoption by unmarried couples is going to be a possibility, the question will arise as to whether the relaxation of the rules will be extended to gay and lesbian couples. The question is not addressed in the Consultation Paper, but has been the subject of a considerable amount of public and media speculation.

Step-parent adoptions were addressed by the Paper. The rationale for this was put thus (para.2.14):

"The step-parent is likely to be effectively sharing responsibility for the care of the child, and the family may wish to seek some legal recognition of the relationship which the step-parent has with the child. Some applications appeared to be based also on a wish for the child to be known by the step-father's surname."

The issues here are legal recognition and identity. In fact, the legal recognition issue could be resolved by means less draconian than adoption. An award of legal custody and guardianship to the step-parent would add him or her to the list of those having legal responsibility for a child, and power to act on the child's behalf, without removing these rights from the non-custodial birth parent.

The issue of the child's surname could also be resolved without resort to adoption, by simply changing the use of the name in a practical way. There is no necessity in Scotland for resort to a deed-poll procedure or an application to the court. The non-custodial parent could challenge a change of name and approach a court to adjudicate on the matter, but all of this could take place outwith the adoption process. Matters of inheritance too could be dealt with through appropriate provisions in wills, although there could be some problems in the event of intestacy.

Adoption is therefore not a necessary legal solution to these issues, and it may not be a desirable one. The Consultation Paper recognised that, whilst it may be appropriate in some cases, in others it would not. It stated (para.2.15):

> "Adoption by a parent and step-parent severs the legal link between a child and the other side of his birth family, including grandparents. It is also possible that the step-parent's family will have little or no interest in the adopted child, so that the child loses one family without really gaining another. Such a situation may be confusing and lead to identity problems for the child, especially if the new marriage breaks down."

This is indeed a considerable possibility. The Paper continued (para.2.19):

> "The relative incidence of breakdown of second and subsequent marriages makes a step-parent adoption particularly vulnerable to the difficulties of divorce or separation. It is even possible that the parent and child may wish to have the child's legal relationship with the other side of the birth family restored. In such situations, it has been suggested that the order should be revocable with the agreement of all the parties, or, where appropriate, the agreement being dispensed with."

This suggestion would, if implemented, put adoption on the same "Yes, but..." basis as marriage, whereby an apparent commitment for life is implicitly watered down into something more potentially finite and controllable. The legal and religious concept of marriage as "the two shall be one", or, "till death us do part", has metamorphosed into a dissoluble contract between two individuals. The initial intention of permanency may be there, but the reality of separation is contemplated and legally facilitated. A move towards revocable adoption orders would mirror that process.

The authors of the Consultation Paper felt that development to be unacceptable. Children need stability, and not mere pious intentions. Speaking of the revocability suggestion, they concluded that (para.2.20):

> "This is not an attractive option. One of the major features of an adoption order is its irrevocability. This feature underlines the fact that it is not simply the responsibility to care for the child which is the issue,

but the right to be regarded in law as the parent of the child with the same permanence given to the child–parent relationship as is enjoyed by birth parents."

The Consultation Paper therefore proposed that, while step-parent adoption should still be available as the most appropriate option for some children, no provision should be made for any specific revocation procedures.

The Role Of Law

The dilemmas discussed above raise issues about the role of the law in relation to changing family structures. Does the law merely acknowledge and respond to changes in family structures, or does it influence them?

I referred earlier to a perception that the law, in providing escape routes for victims of abusive domestic authority, has undermined the structures which that authority – for better or worse – upheld. I would see this social change as an unintentional side-effect of a change in the law.

Sometimes the law does seek to influence family structures, more in the direction of holding back change than initiating it. The Scottish Law Commission considered the argument that (para.16.18):

"to provide an adjustive remedy for cohabitants would be to encourage cohabitation and devalue marriage."

Although, admittedly, the Commission took a common-sense view and was not swayed by the argument.

Politically, there seems to be a move towards re-emphasising the role of the family through provisions such as the Child Support Act 1991, which introduced strong new measures and a whole new agency to bring non-contributing, or insufficiently contributing fathers to heel.

Whilst the financial principle of holding parents to their responsibilities to pay for their children's upkeep seems sound, the Act has been criticised for clinging to that principle without fully taking into account the way families have actually changed, and the way people actually live; the emotional and physical vulnerability of the single parent mother, which can, from her perspective, put her financial deprivation into the shade; the actual fact of second families with human demands equal to those of the first.

There has also been talk of making divorce more difficult, as we become increasingly and uncomfortably aware of the damaging effects on children of their parents' separation. Yet one has to ask what the societal response would be to such a move? Would it encourage more couples to stay together? Would their children actually benefit, given that individual expectations have changed? Or is frustration of these expectations more likely to engender explosive relationships than it was in the days when one party – the vulnerable one – would just knuckle under and stay put, because there were no expectations, and nowhere else to go? Would we really want to return to that kind of society anyway?

I referred earlier to the Convention on the Rights of the Child, and to the declaration in the Preamble that the UN is,

"Convinced that the family, as the fundamental group of society and the natural environment for the growth and well-being of all its members and particularly children, should be afforded the necessary protection and assistance so that it can fully assume its responsibilities within the community,"

The Preamble goes on to recognise that:

"the child, for the full and harmonious development of his or her personality, should grow up in a family environment, in an atmosphere of happiness, love and understanding."

The family environment in itself is not enough; there must be an atmosphere of "happiness, love and understanding."

The State cannot guarantee happiness, love and understanding, though it can do much to minimise some of the barriers to it. If families are to have a future, the State must recognise their changing nature. It must show that it values families, not by means of pious statements, but by devoting valuable resources to support families in the form of day care, respite care, family education and support.

It must acknowledge the existence of tensions and power imbalances within families, by providing more effective escape routes for vulnerable members, rather than a 'hear no evil, see no evil' approach which would tend to sweep the abuses back under the carpet of the well-ordered family. It must promote, so far as it is able, an "atmosphere of happiness, love and understanding."

In conclusion, I return to my introductory reference to the Secretary of State's statement in the Foreword to the White Paper on child care law that

"The law is an essential expression of society's values."

The question that arises today is whether society still values the family, or whether individualism has taken over. Margaret Thatcher, in her infamous and oft-quoted statement to *Woman's Own* magazine on 31 October 1987, said that:

"There is no such thing as Society, there are individual men and women, and there are families."

My contention is that the situation we are facing is one in which there are no such things as families; there are individual men, women and children, and there is Society – the State. It is not a prospect that pleases me. I want there to be a future for families. I think most people do. But they do not want the old repressive notion. They want families founded on respect for the individual, which means that individual men, women and children must acknowledge the need to respect each other. The law must acknowledge that desire and that need, and support families by developing in that direction.

References

Clyde Report (1992) *Report of the Inquiry into the Removal of Children from Orkney in February 1991.* Edinburgh: HMSO.

General Assembly of the United Nations (1989) *The Convention on the Rights of the Child.*

Scottish Law Commission (1992) *Report on Family Law.* Edinburgh: HMSO.

Scottish Office (1993) *Scotland's Children – Proposals for Child Care Policy and Law.* White Paper, Edinburgh: HMSO.

Scottish Office (1993) *The Future of Adoption Law in Scotland.* Consultation Paper issued by the Social Work Services Group, Edinburgh.

5

FAMILIES AND THE FUTURE: THE SCOTTISH DIMENSION

Niall Campbell

Introduction

THE family as an ideal, and as a reality, is at the centre of so much of our policy-making and action. We expect a lot of the family. Yet the family can be approached from many angles. It can be defined in many ways. It remains both obvious and elusive.

My brief is the Scottish dimension to families and the future.

What I would like to do to start with is precisely the opposite. I would like to speak very briefly about Scottish families and the past. This is not to be difficult but to illustrate, in a Scottish context, the way in which the family has changed and is changing. In this way I would like to illustrate one of the key points made right at the start of the White Paper *Scotland's Children*: the changing nature of the family.

Having looked backwards I would then like to look forward. I will address particularly issues about families and children, but also about families and community care and families and offenders.

The main themes will be,

(a) the changing nature of the family,

(b) the high expectations we have of the family, and

(c) the need to do things with families not to them.

One of the words which Scotland has given to the world is "clan". It has a range of associations and in Scotland today is used to describe family in its widest sense of a large number of people who are all assumed to be related because they have the same surname. The family in this sense is particularly strong in Scotland. This is partly because of the huge amount of emigration from Scotland in the nineteenth century.

Yet the word "clan" in Gaelic does not mean "family"; it means "children". This is because Highland families saw themselves as the children of some heroic founder. However, I think it also illustrates the extent to which families in Scotland and elsewhere are defined in terms of children and considered important because of children.

Of course, not all families have children and children become independent of their families. Nevertheless, it is because of the need to consider the needs of children that the institution of the family is considered so important, although this is not just a child care issue, as I shall point out later.

Looking Backwards

It is tempting, but dangerous, to look to the past for contrast or reassurance about the family and to pick out interesting statistics. Much is familiar in general terms and has been described from a United Kingdom point of view by previous speakers. In some aspects Scotland mirrors the rest of the UK and Europe. In other aspects it differs.

Family size in Scotland has been falling steadily over the past 150 years. In 1871 there were 33 live births per 1,000 of the population. In 1931 the figure was 19. Today it is 12. The graph of the number of live births which used to rise like an Alpine range above the foothills of the number of deaths is now very close to the number of deaths. The Scottish population after growing substantially is now static and ageing. This is a European phenomenon.

At the same time, life expectancy of Scottish children has increased dramatically. When my grandfather was born the life expectancy for a male at birth was just over 40. When my sons were born it was 70. I recently visited a museum of childhood in the Highlands. The extracts from the dominie's log of a small rural primary school a century ago were full of records of closures for contagious diseases which were often fatal. On the remote island of St Kilda eight out of ten babies in the mid nineteenth century died of tetanus very soon after birth from the "sickness of eight days" as it was known. There have been huge strides in dealing with childhood illness. Again, a European phenomenon.

Life expectancy is, of course, not only a question of dealing with infant mortality. The good health of families in Scotland depends on us tackling health problems in which Scotland has a particularly bad record. We have the worst record for heart disease and for cancer in the western developed world. The Secretary of State's policy statement "Scotland's Health" sets out action on the Scottish dimension to how we eat, how much we smoke and drink.

These major demographic changes have important effects on families, especially when taken with other social changes. Marriage seems a much more fragile institution. For every two marriages in England and Wales in 1991 there was one divorce. The rate of divorce in Scotland is not, however, as high as that in England and Wales. In Scotland for approaching every three marriages there was one divorce. However, this is twice what it was in 1971.

In Scotland over the last decade the proportion of births outside marriage has more than doubled to one in every three births in 1992 but three-quarters of these were registered by both parents. In the United Kingdom one parent families with dependent children have nearly doubled as a proportion of families with dependent children. Families in this position rose from 10% in 1976 to 19% in 1991.

Yet look further back. Although they varied greatly throughout the country, in some parts of rural Scotland in the nineteenth century illegitimacy rates were over 16%. A minister in Lanarkshire at that time said "I really do not remember when I last married a young woman who was not in the family way".

One can multiply these statistics endlessly. The one lesson one can draw from looking back is how families have varied and keep on varying. Yet children need and want the same thing – stable and reliable parenting and the sense of continuity which flows from that. We cannot predict from the past what is going to happen to the family in the future. But we must look ahead. This is what was done at the start of the White Paper *Scotland's Children*.

Looking Forward

Having looked briefly backwards, I would now like to look forwards as I have been asked. In *Scotland's Children* the family was seen as the essential basis and background to the care and upbringing of children. For that reason the White Paper started with a brief discussion of the family and how changes are affecting children. It tried to look forward to where these trends might take us.

The White Paper points out that throughout Europe children are affected by major social and demographic changes. Children now generally occupy a smaller proportion of the population because of the falling birth rate and the increasing numbers of elderly people. Taking forward the statistics which I mentioned earlier to the year 2011, there will be about 44,000 fewer children in Scotland than there are today. With the increased likelihood of divorce and with, in half of these divorces, one partner being under 21, more younger children are being affected by divorce and separation. Twenty four per cent of all children involved in divorce proceedings in 1991 in Scotland were under 5.

It was pointed out in the White Paper that largely as a consequence of increasing divorce rates, the number of children in Scotland now living in one parent families has risen significantly. In 1980, 44,000 children lived in families receiving one parent benefit. By 1991 the number had almost doubled to 87,000.

The careful work carried out by the National Children's Bureau, which is now allied to Children in Scotland, showed that the more transitions children experience, the more likely they are to report difficulties with school friendships and family relationships. Yet it is, I think, possible to be too gloomy about where the statistics seem to be pointing if they are simply extrapolated.

It is worth remembering that in the United Kingdom in 70% of families the children are living with both their natural parents. Most children of divorced parents do not experience particular difficulties.

The White Paper also touched upon important changes in employment and patterns of employment. The increasing involvement of women in all areas of life has important implications for the family and, in particular, for men, who now take a greater share of the responsibilities of providing care. The White Paper pointed out that the ways in which services are designed and provided need to give men's caring role a greater recognition and support.

However, despite all the changes which have been particularly striking over the past 20 years and no doubt will continue, the White Paper concluded that families remain, and will remain, the foundation of care for children and the development of young people. However, these families will need support in ensuring a consistently high quality of care.

Against this background, the Government stated its belief that the family is of fundamental importance to our society and the Government is committed to providing social welfare services designed to support and assist children within their families so far as this is consistent with the children's welfare.

It may seem strange that we should give such key importance to an institution – the family – which is always changing and which cannot be defined. But I do not think this should worry us. As previous speakers have pointed out, there is no single prescribed form for the family. Children now experience very diverse forms of family life as their parents cohabit, separate, marry and re-marry. Policy making needs to take account of this in ensuring the stability and continuity which children need.

White Paper Principles

It was against that background that the White Paper set out certain key principles. These principles were derived from the United Nations Convention on the Rights of the Child, with its belief that the family is the fundamental group in society within which children grow up. Particularly important within the White Paper are the following principles:

(a) Parents should normally be responsible for the upbringing and care of their children.

(b) Every effort should be made to preserve a child's family home and contacts.

(c) Any intervention in the life of a child or family should be on formally stated grounds, properly justified, in close consultation with all the relevant parties.

Equally important are the principles that every child should be treated as an individual and have the right to express their views about any issues or decisions affecting or worrying them; and that every child has the right to a positive sense of identity.

Thus, running through all the child care principles in the White Paper – and I have not quoted all of them – is the importance of the child and the importance of the family. Yet these may be in conflict. Where there is conflict it is always the child's interests which must be given the greatest consideration. The aim should be to avoid dramatic intervention wherever possible and support the family in coping.

As it was put in the White Paper, parents do not "own" their children. Equally, it was said that public child care law assumes that parents should be free to care for their children without undue interference from the state.

White Paper Implementation

It is all very well to discuss the family and the future in general terms. However, the reason why central government needs to be clear about the family is that it needs to be clear about the legislative and administrative decisions which affect families.

I would like to illustrate this by describing how certain parts of the White Paper are being taken forward in ways which will be important for families in Scotland.

The main purpose of the White Paper was to set out proposals for reform. By no means all that is in the White Paper requires legislation but that will be one of its most important single outcomes. Preparatory work for a broadly based Bill is in hand and the Secretary of State intends to introduce legislation when Parliamentary time is available.

A number of the changes which the White Paper proposed would give added rights and protection to the family when faced with the prospect of intervention by the State.

(a) It was proposed that parental rights orders would require the approval of a court, not just a local authority committee.

(b) It was proposed that if a child is taken to a place of safety, both parent and child would have a new right of appeal to the sheriff.

Yet there are other proposals which are designed to protect the child as an individual:

(a) It was proposed that there should be an exclusion order to exclude the abuser from the family home.

(b) It was proposed that there should be changes to the provisions for children who seek refuge when in particular difficulty or stress.

(c) It was proposed that there would be added emphasis on taking the child's views into account. (Listening to children is an issue to which we are giving increasing attention.)

(d) It was proposed that there would be provision for the parents to be excluded from a children's hearing if the child wants to speak to the panel without the parents being present.

The principles underlying these proposals in the White Paper are the need to protect the family in its dealings with the State but also to protect the child in his or her dealings with the family. These balances have always been difficult to strike. In both relationships the weaker party is being strengthened.

However, you cannot simply legislate to support the family. It is supported in a great range of ways.

I mentioned earlier that practical support is needed for families and children, including especially families with disabled children. At a Scottish level initiatives are being taken to develop child care and family support, particularly in areas of deprivation and through The Scottish Office-led urban partnerships. For instance, the Castlemilk After School Care project caters for school age children whose parents work. The children are looked after before and after school and during holidays – difficult times for families and children where employment may be a key to keeping the family together.

Family And Community Care

As I have mentioned, family life is seen as particularly important in relation to children. Yet families are networks that last for life and I would like to talk about the role of families in community care. We are now talking about families in their widest sense – not simply the nuclear family. Here too the ability of the family to provide care is affected by the demographic and social changes mentioned earlier. People are looking ahead and trying to interpret the trends. Reports are being published with titles like "A Crisis in Care?"

Looking to the future there are two important forces at work both of which affect the family.

First, the proportion of elderly people in the community is going to continue to rise.

Second, the move of vulnerable people – people with mental illness, people with learning disability or physical handicap, frail elderly people – out of institutions and into the community will continue.

More care will be provided by families. But in many cases this cannot be provided without help from outside.

One of the things which healthy families do is to provide care and support for family members. One important reason for the existence of social work services is to provide help for people who don't have families who are able to do this. For a long time there have been public services to help adults who need care and support. But most care comes from members of families or from close friends. The traditional view is that social work steps in when families are not available. But this is not the whole story. We now realise that meeting people's needs is best accomplished by working alongside families in partnership with them. Of course, this is not always easy. Sometimes the needs and wishes of one family member conflict with those of another. For example, in reaching decisions about the independence of young adults with learning difficulties; or for determining the level of acceptable risk for an older person who cannot look after themselves.

Let me give one example of the importance of working in partnership with family members. In many places, the allocation of home helps for particular tasks is only available if there is no relative living with or near to the person in need. However, home help service alongside the support given by family members can often sustain older people longer in their own homes and with a higher quality of life. The provision of support for family members in their caring tasks and the sharing of such tasks between public services and families therefore has a positive outcome both for the person in need and for family members themselves.

In recognition of the importance of carers the Government's community care policy gives prominence to their needs. One of the six key objectives for community care set out in the White Paper *Caring for People* is to provide practical support for carers. Carers also have the right now to an assessment of their own needs and this is increasingly happening. In Scotland, local authorities have embraced this objective with enthusiasm. We see carers support groups, carers forums, carer development officers, carer strategies. All of these developments reflect the recognition of the crucial importance of families in caring for their more needy members.

The commitment to support for carers is also evident in the distribution of public money. At national and local level many organisations for carers are getting support. The Scottish Office gives funding to the Carers' National Association and to Crossroads, two organisations devoted entirely to supporting the needs of carers. We welcome the development of the work of the Princess Royal Trust for Carers in Scotland.

We also support many other initiatives such as a recent grant to develop programmes to support parents and carers of people with profound and complex learning disabilities. Through the Mental Illness Specific Grant we have provided funding for many organisations to support carers, especially in relation to people with dementia. Some of these schemes provide sitting services and sleepover services whereby a paid carer will relieve a family member from their caring responsibilities for perhaps one evening a week. These schemes are extremely highly valued and effective.

The main objectives and elements of the policy have been set out. The main demands can be identified. The difficult job is making it all happen. It is not only a question of resources because significant resources have been made available. It is a question above all of combining imagination and organisation – imagination to look ahead to new ways of providing care, organisation to mobilise the resources of a range of agencies to support the individual and the family.

Particularly important are the following:

(a) Providing individuals and families with information so that they may choose what suits them best. Research which we have recently carried out in various fields of community care shows the importance of developing well presented information.

(b) Providing respite. Our report *The Patchwork Quilt* showed how much there was to be done in this field. Resources have been identified in the community care money for respite care.

(c) Clear care arrangements so that everyone knows where they fit in are also vital. This is particularly important for families. Care management and assessment processes are the key.

In community care as we move away from institutional care, we expect more of families and our policies need to recognise this. But there are very positive sides to this. I recently met, with her daughter, the mother of a girl with learning disabilities. The daughter had just moved to imaginative accommodation in the community run jointly by voluntary and statutory agencies. The mother felt that the years her daughter had spent in an institution had been "lost" years and was looking forward to much more family involvement in her daughter's life.

Offenders and their Families

I would now like to turn to a very different area of stress for families. Apart from the death of a parent, there can scarcely be a more traumatic event for a family than for one of the parents (almost invariably the father) to go to prison. Great financial and emotional strains will be placed on the wife and the children. There are the practical problems of visiting and confronting the rest of the community. There is the difficulty of reintegrating the parent into the family on release.

Although women form only a very small percentage of the prison population at any time (3% of the average daily population in 1992), particular problems may be created for the families of imprisoned women, many of whom are the sole carers of their children. Many of these children will be looked after by other relatives or family friends, whilst others will be subject to formal measures of care through the legal system. All will experience dislocation, disruption and distress.

An important recent initiative in relation to women prisoners has been the development of a collaborative project involving two local authorities, to establish effective pre-release links and throughcare services to women prisoners from Strathclyde who have drugs-related problems. The provision of specialist services in relation to the drugs problems faced by these women should have a very positive impact on their families, and, in particular, their children, by reducing the risk of further drug-related offending by the women.

Where the offender is a child of the family, in their late teens when so much offending takes place, there are other problems of family support. If the young man is to put offending behind him on release, he may well need the support of his family.

Roger Shaw who was a Research Fellow at the Cambridge Institute of Criminology has estimated that in England and Wales 100,000 children each year experience the imprisonment of their fathers. Whilst he has not conducted a comparable study in Scotland, he suggests that the proportion of Scottish children who experience their father being imprisoned may be larger, due to the proportionately greater use of short periods of custody, especially for fine default and remand.

In relation to the latter point, at least, it is hoped that the further development in Scotland of the new Supervised Attendance Order, a court disposal which can be imposed instead of custody in cases of fine default, will go some way towards improving the situation.

Another positive development in Scotland has been the creation of The Scottish Forum on Prisoners and Families, comprising representatives from a wide range of interested parties, which was established in 1991 with the specific purpose of exploring the needs of the families of prisoners, and promoting best practice. The Scottish Office, the Scottish Prison Service, Strathclyde Regional Council and key independent sector organisations such as the Scottish Association for the Care and Resettlement of Offenders, Save the Children Fund and WRVS are all represented on this Group.

In 1992 the Forum commissioned a research report (Peart and Asquith), funded by Save the Children Fund and Scottish Prison Service, which recommended a number of developments to promote the best interests of children and families affected by imprisonment.

One of the most important initiatives to result from this report has been the creation, by the Scottish Prison Service, of the post of Family

Contact Development Officer in every prison. These officers have the particular task of co-ordinating and improving the visiting arrangements in each prison and assisting in the provision of appropriate training for prison staff, to increase their awareness of the range of problems which prisoners' families may face.

In common with all other sections of the population, the families of offenders may seek the assistance of social work departments and other helping agencies in their own right. Increasingly, research suggests that the involvement of family members can be a key element in bringing about positive changes in attitudes and behaviour, and thereby reducing the risk of re-offending. Similarly, research suggests that within the context of probation and other forms of supervision in the community, a greater impact is likely to be made on criminal behaviour if underlying problems such as family relationships, accommodation and finance, are also tackled. The National Standards for social work services in the criminal justice system place clear responsibilities on social work departments to ensure that particular attention is given to addressing such problems in the course of their work with offenders.

Thus the families of offenders are another group of families whose needs and contribution we need to consider.

Families And The Future: The Scottish Dimension

What is the Scottish dimension in all of this and what does the future hold for Scottish families?

As I have mentioned, much of the romanticised history of Scotland is seen in terms of families and clans. Yet in reality it must have been far from the security which we associate with the term family.

The family in this wider sense was the source of great pride. Shortly after the engagement was announced between Queen Victoria's daughter and the Duke of Argyll's son and heir, an English tourist (a common feature of many Scottish stories) was visiting Inveraray – the Campbell capital. He asked one of the locals what he thought of the engagement and received the reply that it must be a proud day for Queen Victoria.

The family has a strong place in Scottish history. It is possible to romanticise it in the past. However, certainly in the present and in the future, the family will remain the key unit. There are both differences and similarities between what is happening to families in Scotland and the rest of the UK. There are some striking differences between families in Scotland and the rest of Europe. There are also some striking similarities.

Most contributors have made clear the recent key changes which have affected Scottish families in the recent past:

(a) falling birth-rates

(b) longer life expectancy

(c) increased divorce rates

(d) increased numbers of single parent families.

Yet, if we look back further in Scottish history, there have always been changes affecting the family. They have been the results of all sorts of forces – energetic public health officers, changing views of morality, technological inventions, surgical advances – all interacting in unexpected ways. We should not take a pessimistic view of the changes. We should be sensitive to them and ready to enable the family to cope.

Social policy continues to be based on confidence in family solutions. Policies are designed to respond to families' desires to look after their own members in the community wherever possible. They also expect quite a lot from families as we move away from institutional solutions. Throughout Scotland one cannot help being aware of the great institutions, often huge baronial structures. Watching the demolition of Woodilee Hospital as one travels by train to Glasgow is a very visible illustration of the move away from institutional solutions. We are now moving away from such solutions in many areas of what we do.

In 1976 there were 6,336 children in residential care. Today there is a third of that number. In 1979 there were 6,656 people with learning disabilities in hospitals. Today there is two-thirds of that number.

But Scotland has not moved at the same rate as England in this process, particularly in the community care field. What is important is to continue this process in a well prepared way, recognising the role of families in making it successful by ensuring the right kind of support for them.

Conclusion

While Scotland shares with other countries many of the changes which are affecting the family, it is also different. It has its own special characteristics. There is a Scottish dimension. Family has been important in the past.

More importantly the family, with all its variety and capacity for change, will continue to be the key to the future, providing a source of continuity and stability for all its members.

References

Peart, K. and Asquith, S. (1993) *Prisoners and Their Families:* Scottish Forum on Prisoners Families 1993.

Pugh, G. (ed.) 1993 *Thirty Years of Change for Children:* National Children's Bureau.

Scotland's Childrens: (Cm 2286) HMSO 1993.

Shaw, R. (1992) *Prisoners' Children: What are the issues?* MacMillan.
Smout, T.C. (1986) *A Century of the Scottish People 1830-1950:* Collins.
Steel, T. (1975) *The Life and Death of St Kilda:* Fontana.

6

FAMILIES AND THE FUTURE: THE SOCIAL WORK DIMENSION

Mary Hartnoll

Introduction

DR Samuel Johnson's Dictionary (1826 edition) gives 3 definitions of 'family'. Swift defined a family as those who live in the same house. The Old Testament definition was those who descend from one common progenitor. And Bacon defined it as a class, a tribe or a species.

Today there is still no single definition of a family and what we call a traditional family has a relatively short history in human terms. Yet in social policy terms, the assumptions we make about family life are fundamental to our future. The timing of this conference is therefore welcome. Social work is rooted in the needs of society and must adapt its response to meet changing need. Assumptions about family life are at the heart of a series of changes being made – in health, education, housing and social security – and for social work in community care, criminal justice and child care. Some of the changes are by government in terms of legislation and finance. But many of the changes are economic, particularly in work patterns and environmental issues.

In this chapter I intend to identify some broad themes which have particular importance for social work over the next ten years and then bring out my crystal ball for some more speculative thoughts about social work and families in the next century.

Changes In The Family

If we define family in terms of parents and children, the structure of the family in Europe and in Scotland is changing. The average age of mothers having their first child is rising. The percentage of the population under 16 is falling. The percentage of babies born outside marriage has risen dramatically. Divorce rates are rising, though more slowly in Scotland than in the rest of the United Kingdom. In Strathclyde one in four families is cared for by a lone parent and in Glasgow, the figure rises to one in 3 – the majority of whom are women.

Across all northern European countries the number of women in paid work is rising. In the United Kingdom the figure is 60% including part-time work. Amongst lone parents the figure is lower – in Strathclyde it is only 29% – although that is more to do with shortage of opportunity rather than choice.

If we turn the figures round, there are still 40% of children being brought up in traditional families. Marriage remains popular and many of those who divorce re-marry. Many cohabitations are stable. Michael Anderson in *Today's Family in Historical Context* comments that there has always been a looming crisis in family relationships.

Many of the social problems highlighted by the media, academics and politicians have been recurrent throughout the centuries. The survey by the National Children's Bureau of people born in March 1958 reported that the people surveyed had by and large at the age of 33, discarded traditional models of family life, opting to cohabit, divorce and produce children outwith wedlock. The survey also suggests they felt they were happier. We have to be careful not to equate change with problems. Changes in family structures can be beneficial. People are living longer and have different expectations within marriage. The cultural patterns are more varied with many members of black and ethnic minority communities having different family structures and values.

The facts of change in family structure can therefore be demonstrated. Whether the changes in themselves are good or bad for children and families is another question. The underlying problem is that the social changes have come at a time of economic upheaval. The increase in unemployment, the lack of jobs particularly for those without skills, the dependence on economic growth to keep pace with our neighbours in Europe, have accompanied the changes in family life.

Social policy in responding to these changes has emphasised the values of parental responsibility and market forces. Little has been done to help women combine employment and child rearing. If we include the extended family, the increasing number of very old people has placed extra demands on families, especially on women. Surveys of how families divide duties suggest that women still carry the main burden of caring and housework as well as an increasing role as breadwinner. There is an assumption that families will also care for children with special needs, with young people who have received head or spinal injuries in accidents and for relatives discharged from hospital. Advances in medical skill have brought benefits but have also added to the pressure on families.

If social policy had been geared to supporting the changes in the economic system, to the changes brought by medical skill, to the increased number of elderly people, then perhaps the earning capacity of the country might have grown to fund some of the services required. As it is, the very real financial difficulties facing the country led to a tightening of constraints on social security and on services provided by social work at a time when the need for those services was increasing.

Against this background of the developing role of social work and how it adapts modern social work in Scotland has its roots in the 1960s. The Kilbrandon Report and subsequent Rowntree paper led on to the Social Work (Scotland) Act with its bold and optimistic approach.

The emphasis was clearly on prevention, engagement with families and on acting as change agent with communities.

Looking back, it is remarkable what was achieved with the resources available. There were criticisms, but a wide range of new community initiatives began. There was growth in services but most had started from a very low base. The Children's Hearing System was perceived for a time as a soft option but when it was reviewed, widespread support emerged for its approach. There was however continued questioning about the role of social work.

The Barclay Report of 1982 produced two critiques that mirrored the public debate about the role of social work. The first is expressed in the words of David Jones: "The problem with...the conception of a community based family oriented service is not that it has been proved inadequate but that it has never been tried."

The opposite view – expressed by Professor Robert Pinker – was that social work should have a less ambitious set of goals rather than looking for needs in the community at large.

For a time, we concentrated on this more limited agenda. Social work depends on society for its continued existence. It must fulfil the needs of society as perceived by policy makers and most users of our services. We have developed targets and objectives, established planning systems and engaged in consultation. The confidence expressed in social work by the Community Care legislation can be seen however as a recognition that what is really needed is a service that believes in the community-based, family-oriented service that had been so much criticised.

Any discussion of social work must take account of the ambivalence with which we are viewed. Constant criticism and sceptical scrutiny can be debilitating for social workers. But even more serious is the stigma that it brings for users. The most published criticism of social work arises from individual cases and sometimes the criticism is valid. But some of the most vocal criticism is when social work is properly carrying out the work it is required in legislation to undertake. I do not anticipate that there will be any change in the public view of social work over the next decade. I hope though that we can continue to offer an integrated family-based service as I still believe it will make the best use of scarce resources and avoid some of the worst effects of stigma.

Family change and social policy

I want to look at the way in which some of the changes in family structure now require a change in social policy if social work is to have any chance of carrying out the duties that the country, through Parliament, has given to us.

Five themes of family change will be considered and the implications for social work over the next decade will also be considered. These five themes are:

a) The increasing economic divide between the rich and the poor
b) The changing aspirations of people especially women
c) The change in the population structure
d) The increased diversity of family structures
e) The implications of legislative change.

Family Change – increased divide between rich and poor

The emphasis on market forces and personal responsibility is inevitably accompanied by the belief that under-achievement is a personal failure. While all policy makers would recognise the need to balance levels of benefit with reasonable work incentives, it is manifestly unfair to blame the majority of people who lose their jobs for the economic changes that are taking place.

For children brought up in families living in poverty and for young people facing a 50% rate of unemployment in their area, the future is very different from that of children brought up in financially secure families where skill development and educational opportunities can give extra support to young people. Families can disintegrate in all sectors of society but more children will come into public care from poor families and from lone parent families. One of the hardest critiques of social work to answer is that of balancing the needs of people who are just managing with the duty of giving support to those who cannot manage. For example, it is argued that if families were given half the resources devoted to substitute placements, there would be fewer children received into care. A similar argument is used in relation to youth homelessness. Social Work has a responsibility to young people who have been in care – but what is really the difference between them and a youngster of 16 who has never been in care? He is just as homeless when he is told to leave after a family row.

There is no easy answer. We are dealing constantly with people at the threshold of care. When pressures on families change, the numbers at the threshold will increase.

Social work never operates in isolation. Changes in the social security system which are aimed at reducing public expenditure rather than problem solving will add to need for social work resources both for people in care and for those who are just not coping.

There are benefit systems which can be targeted at particular needs and which do offer people incentives. Some of the legislation around disability has given people more control over the services they need. The role of social work in giving people good information and access to every benefit and service to which they may be entitled has increased over the past decade. Social work cannot and should not take on the task of resolving the problems of poverty in families. In child care it has to concentrate services on those children who should and could remain with their family. It must go on helping local communities provide some of the supporting services they need.

Family Change – Changing Aspirations

The second change I want to consider is that of changing aspirations. There is a link with the first issue because it is likely that changing aspirations can only be a reality for those who are becoming more affluent. Those who are poor have few options. Of particular importance for social work in working with families in the future is the changing attitude around the role of women. Social work depends on the traditional role of women. There is some change but still the majority of carers are women. We depend on women to come forward as foster carers.

There are certain stereotypes of women and womanhood in the public eye. Most social workers are women. Most care staff are women.

Home helps evoke positive thoughts of women as practical, looking after others and using common sense. In the child sexual abuse cases that have had a high profile, despite social workers working with police, it is social work that has borne the brunt of public attack. It seems that the use of authority by social workers confronts the stereotype of caring and the role of women.

The shortage of women in management roles in social work is well documented. From 59% women in first line management posts in Scotland, the percentage drops to 26% in senior management – and that is significantly better than in England and Wales. Social work has to adjust to the changing aspirations of women. The ability to adjust will be helped by ensuring there are women in positions of responsibility at all levels in the organisation. The ownership of women's issues has to be shared by men and women. There are many examples of how a recognition of gender issues is beginning to affect how social workers carry out their duties. I want to examine just two of them.

My first example is in the field of child sexual abuse. The extent of the problem of the sexual abuse of children began to emerge during the 1980s. We are still facing denial of the existence of a problem while, at the same time, beginning to face some of its implications. We began by thinking it was a serious but fairly rare occurrence. We know now that there are men who target vulnerable women with young children. There are men in positions of trust in caring agencies who use their position to abuse children.

We are finding the abuse of children is part of a wider problem of violence within the family. We also know that it is in a minority of cases that women are directly involved in the abuse of their children. More women who have not abused their children – though they may not have protected them – however traumatised by their own abuse or their situation, could be helped to continue caring safely for their children. The implications of this for practice are immense. There is some evidence that direct work with children can be very effective but how can we be sure that the intervention will not of itself bring more risk? We have as yet no way of predicting which men will abuse children. When we select foster carers or residential staff or day care staff, if there is no previous conviction and not even their wives or partners have any idea that they have or may abuse children, how can social workers know? Over the next decade, social work has to recognise the implications for family life of the level of abuse, improve its skills in recognising it and develop responses which work with whatever strengths there are in the family. This could potentially mean a move away from such a close identification with the investigative process, so that our role is more concentrated on direct work within the family. We must listen to young people who have been abused and evaluate our intervention so that we can build a good practice that is already developing.

My second example of the response of social work to the changing aspirations of women is in responding to carers. It has been carers themselves – mostly women – who have begun to articulate their needs. I have already mentioned the increased demands on carers by improvements in health care, the increased need for long term support for people with disabilities and the increased number of older people. We have some evidence that men who are lone carers receive more support than lone women carers.

Social work has been responsive in listening to carers. There is recognition of the anger and frustration of women about the position they find themselves in. There are changes in policy and practice. The problem is now essentially one of resources. We know that the marital breakdown rate is higher for families with a multiple handicapped child. The unrelieved burden of caring adversely affects both parents' physical and mental health.

The quality of life for the family – the parents, the brothers and sisters and the extended family – can be improved immensely by good quality respite care, day care and home care. But the cost of these will not equate in savings in long term hospital or residential care. Whether or not we believe there is such a thing as Society, the values of social work recognise that we have a mutual responsibility to share in looking after people with profound handicaps – some of them resulting from those same improvements in health care that have benefited all of us. Care in the community is about sharing care – not leaving it all to the family. That costs money.

These are two examples of increased expectations in respect of women. It is not just in respect of women's issues that expectations are changing. There are other issues on which aspirations of families are changing which will have major implications for the future pattern of social work, for example, the growth in advocacy and the expectation to be involved. There are also increased expectations in terms of standards of services and in their availability.

Social workers need to be clear when they are having to ration resources. There has been an outcry lately about doctors using computers to decide who they will treat or making decisions based on age. The underlying problem is the same.

We must over the next decade in social work identify priorities and engage in public debate about what criteria we are using.

Family Change – Population Structure

The third change in the family which I want to consider is the change in the structure of the population. What are the implications for social work of the decreasing proportion of children and the increasing number of elderly people. The proportion of the dependent population will increase. The ratio of people working who can support those who are dependent will decrease. One response by the government is to consider fiscal means to encourage people to defer retiring – and that may be logical. For social work though it would be some major challenges. Older, newly retired people are a significant resource in terms of voluntary work.

Although it is over 85s who make the greatest demand on social work services, the needs of people aged 60–85 increase significantly and most are currently being met by carers or by friends who are of similar age. A change in expectation around retirement must be thought through.

The complexity of forecasting population change is illustrated in the problems confronted by the United Nations conference on population in Cairo. What the Cairo conference has done is make people think hard about little understood issues – links between population growth, development and education. There are no easy answers but at least the United Nations is trying to make us confront intelligently, the great global trends. Social work in its role of adapting to the needs of people must contribute its knowledge to the debate.

Family Change – Cultural Diversity

Simple societies share a common understanding of what constitutes a family. The complexity of a modern developed society means there is no shared understanding of family. We do not even have words to describe some of the relationships that children have to cope with. Women talk about ex-husbands or ex-partners. What do children call an ex-partner?

We have diversity of family structure through families from black and ethnic minorities. There will be differences in expectation between the different generations. Throughout our history, there has been movement between different cultures, different countries and different continents. As within families, it is often those nearest to us that create the greatest conflict – for example between Scotland and England!

We know from history that racial harmony can most readily be achieved when there is economic prosperity and social cohesion. Problems increase in times of economic decline and social unrest. Social work must increase its understanding of racial discrimination at a time when the need for mutual trust will increase if we are to avoid an escalation of difficulties. We need clear strategies that reflect our values. It can no longer be said that because some groups do not use services, they have different needs. If we identify a low level of usage – for example of home care service – we should consult with the local community to identify what the issues are. It may be a need for information about services or for social work to change the way a service is delivered. Social work has a history of responding, however inadequately at times, to institutional disadvantage and over the next decade, it must work actively with families in ethnic minorities.

There are many other examples of the consequence of diversity of family life. There are lesbian couples bringing up children. There are complex reconstituted families. Because social work is often involved in cases which become public, there can again be an identification of social work as being the cause of what is seen as a problem. We usually cannot respond on the individual case but we must continue to work with families whatever their composition.

Families Change – Legislation

Legislation is often introduced in response to changes in families. The intention behind the legislation will reflect current social policy. The outcome may be beneficial or disastrous as it affects families. The likelihood is that the consequences will not have been anticipated. The recent inquiry by the Mental Health Foundation did not include Scotland but its conclusions are just as important to us. The inquiry was chaired by Sir William Utting, formerly the Chief Inspector of Social Services. The report identifies how the Home Office prison policy did not examine its impact on mentally ill people. The *Independent* in reviewing the report comments, "The deeds of one minister seem to undo those of another. One minister's policy can leave individuals homeless or without benefit."

Several studies suggest a link between cutting income support for young people and the increased number of young offender institutions. We are hoping that there will be a Scottish Children's Bill in the next session of Parliament. I will welcome it particularly as it will clarify responsibility for young people who have been in care. But one issue that greatly exercised us in the Child Care Law Review was that of children in care and education. It was a serious issue at the time of the Kilbrandon Report. Repeated studies have shown how badly children in care perform in terms of education and subsequent employment.

Anyone who has received a child into care has no doubt at all about the total disruption it causes a child in all areas of his life including education. Think of how carefully most parents moving house consider the implications for the child of a change of schooling and the efforts they make to minimise the damage. Yet, despite recognition of the severity of the problem for children in care who may move several times, the recent changes in the education system will continue to increase the pressure on schools to exclude disruptive children or children with special needs. We have evidence that the problem is worsening. Choice for one can mean less choice for others.

There is little coherence in legislation as it affects children and families. The new legislation is only intended to address a limited range of issues. It proved difficult to cross the boundaries between public and private law in one Bill. Children from families in difficulty may be subject to differing legal processes. Even when there is agreement about objectives finding ways of simplifying the decision-making process proved complex.

The Children Act in England and Wales has attempted to provide better child protection and to support the rights of parents. Some of the commentators are now suggesting these aims are incompatible. Fox Harding suggests, "this is a denial of conflict, an attempt to avoid the awkward dilemmas which the child care field inevitably throws up"! The process of resolving conflict is increasingly left to the courts. The inevitable result is the lengthening processes. I was taught that babies should not be moved except in dire emergencies. Children are now being left in limbo for months and years while adults argue about their future.

It is perhaps no coincidence that children's rights are being empha-sised. It sometimes seems that we emphasise rights at the same time as we erode them. On a more positive note however, there is in Scotland greater coherence about how we deal with young people under the age of 16. So in concluding this section of my paper, I have looked at the future of the family in terms of its implications for social work. Most of the issues I have identified are not new. They are contained within the present and rooted within the past. It may be that the changes in the family of themselves do not have as many implications for social work as the accompanying changes in social policy and legislation. There is never a good time to reorganise local government, but for social work, the timing could not be worse. The most complex changes for 30 years are being made in the boundaries between social care and health care and at the same time a new Children's Bill may be introduced. Over the next 5 years, the upheaval of reorganisation will have more impact on our services than all the changing needs of families.

Crystal Ball

Briefly in this final section, I want to get out my crystal ball and raise just three issues with implications for social work into the next century.

Practices Around Fertility

The first concerns the changes that are taking place in the treatment of infertility. Recently there have been some adoption cases that are raising major questions about the nature of adoption and feelings about origins. Feelings about infertility are also deeply felt. Children born as a result of donor insemination or by surrogate parenting or other methods will have to resolve feelings around their origins and identity. In evolutionary terms, it seems possible that there could be an increased chance of infertility amongst this group because of their genetic inheritance. We have seen an increase in the demand for post-adoption services. I would anticipate a growth in demand for services for young people and adults born as the result of these new techniques.

A second change with major implications for all services including social work is the impact of AIDS. Numbers currently are still small. A group of carers that I met recently talked abut the stigma of HIV infection and their isolation. One said that neighbours would no longer come into the house to take a cup of tea and her younger son had been bullied at school. They had to move to an area where no-one knew them. Their infected son needed their care but they themselves needed support.

The third issue which is also already with us is the issue of drugs. I see little likelihood of radical changes in law over the next decade but if the use of illegal drugs continues to grow, the system of control will break down. At the same time, I would anticipate a review of practice in the use of prescribed drugs, partly because of the unforeseen consequences. Drugs, both legal and illegal, have had an enormous impact on family life over the past 50 years. Changes in their use will affect all of us.

Conclusion

A final thought. Maybe we should have not started with the future of the family. The *Independent on Sunday* ran a series asking famous people to choose a book which had changed them. Barbara Castle chose William Morris's poems and in particular 'The Message of March Wind'. In other writing he talked of satisfaction in one's work as the key to happiness. It is economic factors that often dictate the pattern of family life. I have been reading Christian Watt's papers. A strong sense of family runs through the writing of this extraordinary woman who was born in 1833 in a fishing community in the north of Scotland. When she died aged 90 in Royal Cornhill Hospital she had spent nearly half her life there. Her writings are full of interest but above all it is the effect of her work that matters.

Barbara Castle in her note said the writings of Morris toughened her whole thinking. Beauty cannot be appliquéed on to institutionalised ugliness as a preserve of an elite. It must be built into the way people earn their living, their economic and human relationships.

References

Barclay Report (1982) *Social Workers: their role and their tasks* London, Bedford Square Press.

Fox-Harding, L. (1991) *Perspectives in Child Care* Longman.

Fraser, Sir D. (1988) *The Christian Watt Papers* Collieston Caledonian.

Kilbrandon Report (1964) *Report of the Committee on Children and Young people (Scotland)*.

Review of Child Care Law (1990) The Scottish Office.

7

FAMILIES, THE CHILD SUPPORT ACT AND THE WELFARE STATE

Fran Wasoff

THE Child Support Act has been called by the Social Security Select Committee 'the most far-reaching social reform to be made for 40 years'. Its significance for family policy and for low-income families in particular can hardly be overstated. It has been highly controversial and hardly out of the news. Few measures of the present Government, with the possible exception of the poll tax and school testing, have met with such widespread public resistance. Yet unlike the poll tax and school testing, the outcry against the child support reforms was not anticipated by any of the political parties who all gave it their support; Parliamentary debate surrounding it was minimal. In the less than one and a half years that the Act has been in force, it has been the focus of attention of the Social Security Select Committee on several occasions, caused MPs' surgeries to be inundated with complaints, and mobilised battalions of absent parents into demonstrations and displays bordering on civil disobedience. The Government was forced to modify the Act in February of this year, less than a year since it came into force, though its concessions to absent parents failed to appease them. The first Annual Report of the Child Support Agency, published in July, was a catalogue of missed targets and failed objectives. Only this month, the beleaguered Ros Hepplewhite resigned as Chief Executive of the Child Support Agency. Many would now regard the child support reform as a political 'own goal'. How remarkable this should happen to a reform whose underlying principle is one almost everyone supports: that both parents, parents with care *and* absent parents, should support *all* their children to the best of their ability and as a high priority, even if the relationship that produced them has broken down.

In this chapter, I intend to offer some reflections on the Child Support Act as an example of a number of government measures intended to further its ideological agenda of 'strengthening the family' and to consider what might be its impact on the welfare state and on the support individuals and families can expect from society generally. But first I would like to review the context for child support and to briefly sketch its main provisions.

The ideological roots of the Child Support Act can be traced to Margaret Thatcher, in a talk to the National Children's Homes in January 1990, who announced:

"No father should be able to escape from his responsibility and that is why the Government is looking at ways of strengthening the system for tracing an absent father and making arrangements for recovering maintenance more effective."

Later that year, she echoed this theme again with her statement to the 300 Group:

"Government too must be concerned to see parents accept responsibility for their children. For even though marriages may break down, parenthood is for life. Legislation cannot make irresponsible parents responsible. But it can and must ensure that absent parents pay maintenance for their children. It is not fair for them to expect other families to foot their bills too."

Her views were widely shared in Government and in the Conservative Party, but finally the reform itself must be credited to the Major Government.

Although I would not suggest that the Government has anything as coherent as 'a family policy', the child support reforms, together with other policies meant to 'strengthen the family' will have a profound impact on family life. The other reforms I have in mind are community care, encouraging more private provision of pensions, removing young peoples' independent entitlement to benefit, and changes to student grants and loans. All of these reforms have elements in common, and taken collectively will, I believe, redefine the boundaries of public and private obligations of support. They all place greater burdens of support on families, and reduce the support available from the state. Reforms such as these could be said to *privatise* obligations of support, and are in tune with the Government's mission to roll back the boundaries of the state in all aspects of social and economic life.

One might think that rolling back the state might increase families' freedom and flexibility, but it is a feature of this reform that it increases the burdens on families at the same time as reducing their freedom to make their own tailor-made and flexible arrangements. Child support reduces the support that families in difficulty can expect from the state and at the same time increases the power of the state to determine the scale and nature of support families must provide for themselves. Thus, while support may be privatised, the state has had a greater impact than ever before on family life, first by withdrawing support and second by intervening to regulate and determine private agreements once support has been withdrawn. It is also a policy that alters the functions of the welfare state, providing less insurance against common events in family life.

Before I go on to develop these points in greater detail, I would like first to set the context for the child support reforms and to sketch its relevant provisions.

The Context For Child Support: The Growth In Divorce And Lone Parenthood

As most of you will be aware, there has been a substantial growth in the divorce rate which has doubled in the 1970s and which has plateaued in the late 1980s to 12,394 divorces in Scotland in 1991. There are about four divorces to every ten marriages and one in four or five children will experience their own parents divorce before they are 16. In Scotland, about 10,000 children a year are affected by their parents' divorce (Morris et al, p3) .

Over a similar period, there has also been a two fold increase since 1971 in the number of lone parent families. There are now more than one million lone parent families in Britain, about one in five families (OPCS 1993; GHS 1993). Over 90% of these are women and over half of them are divorced or separated. A further quarter of the total is made up of single, 'never married' mothers. (Haskey 1993; Bradshaw and Millar 1991; Holtermann 1993; Burghes 1990). In Scotland in 1991, there were 219,010 lone parent families out of 1,379,940 families in total. (OPCS 1993)

The Growth in Lone Parenthood in Britain: 1971 – 1989

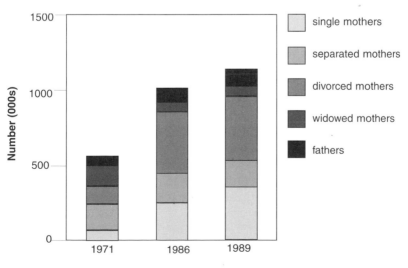

Source: Burghes (1993). p. 6

Growth In Social Security Expenditure On Lone Parents

The child support reforms are particularly significant for lone parent families, since as a group they are highly dependent for their income on means-tested social security benefits. About three-quarters of lone mothers (933,000) get Income Support (IS), 190,100 [15%] receive Family Credit (FC) and less than 300 [<.1%] are in receipt of Disability Working Allowance (DWA) (DSS 1994; 3-5, 15-18). This gives a total of about 90% of lone parents receiving a benefit relevant for child support. Thus, only about 10% of all lone parents during any given year are not in receipt of one of the three relevant means-tested benefits.

Lone Parent Families & Welfare Benefits

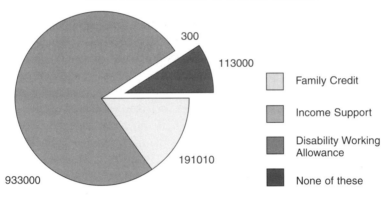

Source: Garnham & Knights (1994)

Lone parent families also predominate in the number of families on benefit. As a proportion of *all* families on IS, lone parents predominate, although they comprise less than 1 in 5 of all families with dependent children. Out of a total of 1,623,000 families on Income Support with a qualifying child in terms of the Child Support Act 1991, 65% are lone parents (CPAG 1994; 18). Lone mothers comprise 40% of all families on FC (DSS 1994;3). They predominate even more amongst families on benefit with qualifying children. Of the 1,305,331 families on a relevant benefit with a qualifying child, 95% are lone parents (CPAG 1994; 18).

However, the proportion of lone parents on benefit receiving maintenance payments has declined. A DSS survey found that only 29% were receiving regular maintenance payments and only 39% had ever received maintenance. It also found that 72% of lone mothers were in receipt of Income Support and 85% had received Income Support at some time since becoming a lone parent. The proportion of lone parents receiving income support who also received maintenance had declined from 50% in 1979 to 23% in 1989. There was also a declining proportion of lone parents in paid employment. Research in Scotland showed that the private system of support on divorce, essentially child support, was declining in importance (Morris et al 1993) and supports the conclusion that maintenance awards by the courts were too low, too inconsistent and too seldom awarded and paid.

Thus lone parents were heading some of the poorest households, most dependent on state benefit and had become less and less reliant for support from an ex-partner or from their own earnings. Not surprisingly, the total social security bill for this group was large and increasing. In 1988/89, the cost of social security to lone parents was reported by the DSS as £3.2 billion, compared with £1.4 billion in 1981/82.

It is clear that the great majority of lone parents likely to be affected by the Child Support Act 1991 are lone mothers on benefit and primarily those on Income Support. As we shall see shortly, child support and entitlement to benefit are closely intertwined, so that we can justifiably view child support as a welfare state income support policy, rather than simply one that governs private arrangements between parents who live apart.

The Child Support Act 1991: Summary Of Provisions

I should like now to sketch some of the key provisions of The Child Support Act: the establishment of an executive agency to administer it, the formula for assessing child support, and the associated changes to means-tested social security benefits.

The Child Support Agency

The Act also established the Child Support Agency, an executive 'next steps' agency accountable to the Secretary of State for Social Security which has the responsibility to assess, collect and enforce maintenance. The Agency has extensive powers for requiring disclosure of information concerning absent parents, for assessment, collection, and enforcement and carrying out reviews. It operates largely along the lines of the old DSS 'liable relatives' scheme and has taken over most of the child support-related work of the courts. There a right to an internal review of the decision of a child support officer and following this, a right of appeal to a Child Support Appeal Tribunal, part of the Independent Tribunal Service.

Maintenance Assessments

A mother (or father) in receipt of means-tested social security benefits (IS, FC, DWA) who is a "parent with care" in terms of the 1991 Act is *required* to apply for a maintenance assessment by a child support officer. If they fail to co-operate without good cause, they risk facing a benefit penalty. Others, whether 'a parent with care' or an 'absent parent' *may* (voluntarily) apply to have child support levels determined by a maintenance assessment by a child support officer. A standard formula is used to determine a sum which then becomes legally binding on the other parent. Once assessed, child support can then be collected and enforced by the Child Support Agency. This is now the only way that is legally binding for a parent with care to obtain aliment from a child's absent parent; the role of the courts in such matters has largely ended, with a significant exception.

There is a transitional period until 1996/97 for parents who both do not receive a relevant benefit and already had a legally-binding maintenance agreement when the Child Support Act came into force. In this case civil courts retain jurisdiction and such a parent may not use the Child Support Agency, even though she would stand to gain the most from this reform. However, if a parent with care applies for Income Support, Family Credit or Disability Working Allowance, the aliment provision of any pre-existing legally-binding agreement becomes unenforceable. In this respect, the Child Support Act is retrospective legislation since it overrides pre-existing legally-binding agreements between ex-partners, even if part of that agreement has already been honoured. Much of the resistance to the Act has centred on the overturning of these 'clean break' agreements or privately negotiated agreements that may have been amicable settlements juggling a number of aspects in the best interests of all.

The Formula: Key Details

The objectives of the formula are :

- to increase the amount, consistency and compliance rates of child support
- to reduce public expenditure on income support and
- to 'encourage' or force more lone parents out to work.

The child support formula determines how much of an absent parent's income (and where relevant, the income of the parent with care) is available for child support. The maintenance requirement is a standard formula based on income support rates. It is determined by household composition and income, and includes a sum to meet the costs of the caring parent. There is little discretion in its application. Because child support is deemed to be a high priority claim on an absent parent's income, many expenses an absent parent regards as essential are not taken into account when an assessment is made. Many complaints have been made that the formula does not have regard to absent parents' existing financial commitments, such as debts, travel to work costs and costs of maintaining access to the children they are obliged to support and costs of support for second families. However, an assessment is meant to leave an absent parent with at least a 'protected income' which is a margin above Income Support levels, so as to retain a work incentive and ensure that another family is not forced onto means-tested benefits (Wasoff 1992).

Figure 1: Child Support Assessment

Q: How much of the absent parent's income is available for child support?

A: The smallest of these three sums:
  • his share of the Maintenance Requirement (MR)
  • up to half his assessable income (A x P)
  • Net income (N) less Protected Income
  • *but* most absent parents must pay a minimum of £2.28 per week.

The amount of child support an absent parent must pay is up to the maintenance requirement but no more than half their assessable income and leaving them with at least a protected level of income. Thus it is the *smallest* of these sums: (his share of).

Changes To Means Tested Benefits

Associated changes have been made to means-tested social security benefits, which not only provide incentives for those in paid work and impose penalties for those not in work, but also act as an inducement for parents with care to seek full-time paid employment. These are:
  • the disregard of maintenance up to £15 per week for lone parents in receipt of Family Credit
  • the reduction (to 16 hours per week) to the minimum number of hours parents must work to be eligible to claim Family Credit
  • a child care allowance for those in receipt of Family Credit, worth up to £28 net for 'allowable' child care costs, from October 1994
  • absent parents receiving Income Support themselves must still pay a minimum sum in child support (now £2.28 pw), and
  • some of a single mother's Income Support may be withheld if she refuses to co-operate with the Child Support Agency in securing child support, without good cause.

The Child Support Act And The Welfare State

I would like to look now at the effect of the child support reforms on some of the functions of the welfare state, particularly in terms of its effects on what is described as horizontal and vertical equity. As John Hills has noted in his review of the debate on the future of the welfare state:

> "The welfare state does more than just relieve poverty. Taking into account the taxes that finance it, the welfare state does redistribute between rich and poor, but also smoothes out income over the life cycle for people with average incomes, acting as a kind of 'savings bank' and evens out income between men and women." (Joseph Rowntree Foundation *Future of Welfare* summary, November 1993; pp 2–3.)

Vertical and horizontal equity are useful concepts in appreciating the variety of functions of a welfare system. Vertical equity is about redistributing resources from richer to poorer people in order to reduce inequalities in income and wealth, and is to a certain extent concerned with the relief of poverty. To the extent that income tax is progressive, it is about vertical equity. Income Support is an example of a benefit that achieves vertical redistribution.

Horizontal equity is concerned with distributing the burdens of social support at a given time across a wide range of social groups. For example, child benefit reduces the cost to individual parents of raising children and spreads it horizontally to other citizens who are not raising children at the time. Income support, though primarily intended for vertical redistribution, can also be seen as a horizontal transfer inasmuch as it transfers resources from two parent families and childless families to one parent families. Horizontal equity can also be seen longitudinally as transferring resources over time and across an individual's life cycle, from times of plenty to times of want. Pensions are an obvious example of this, where an individual contributes during his or her working life and draws on those contributions later in life. Thus, John Hills identifies these five aims for welfare services:

- relief of poverty and redistribution for the long term poor
- insurance against life's risks, like unemployment, family breakdown
- redistribution to particular groups with greater needs, such as for family circumstances, medical care or disability
- smoothing out the level of income over the life cycle
- stepping in where the family 'fails' or cannot provide care itself, for instance, by a redistributive mechanism where women are left alone after divorce. (John Hills, (1993), *The Future of Welfare*, York: Joseph Rowntree Foundation, p 15.)

Let us consider the Child Support Act in relation to each of these aims.

Relief Of Poverty And Redistribution For The Long Term Poor Or To Particular Groups With Greater Needs

Child support is likely to replace at least some public expenditure on income support for long term poor lone parents, and therefore the burden of relief of poverty will fall more on individual former partners and less on society generally. Thus the welfare state will lose some of its present function for the relief of the poverty of lone parents, which, as their high degree of dependency on Income Support shows, is considerable. The welfare state itself will be less vertically redistributive.

As child support is presently constituted, this will do little to improve the degree of poverty relief for lone parents on income support, since for almost all, each £ of child support will result in a corresponding £ reduction in benefit, leaving them no better off: in effect a marginal 'taxation' rate of 100%. Some may well be worse off, since they may face a loss of benefits in kind from absent parents and from social security. For example, lone parents with mortgages whose child support is sufficient to float them off income support could be substantially worse off since they will lose their entitlement to housing benefit to meet mortgage interest payments. Lone parents in future may find their ex-partners are unwilling to concede their share in the matrimonial home, since this can no longer be off-set by a reduction in child support. [Given the very high recovery costs reported by the Child Support Agency, it remains to be seen how much public expenditure savings will actually be achieved (Child Support Agency 1994).]

For some lone parents receiving Family Credit, some enhancement of low income may be realised from the maintenance disregard or from the child care allowance. Child support may encourage some lone parents on income support to seek paid employment plus Family Credit, thereby providing some poverty relief. The research evidence for this is not clear. On the one hand, research by McKay and Marsh (1994) suggests the work incentive effect of a disregard of earnings for lone mothers on Income Support is modest. On the other hand, their research shows that, before the Child Support Act came into force, maintenance was a significantly associated with lone parents seeking paid work.

Insurance Against Life's Risks

Alistair Burt, MP stated earlier in this book that, in his view, the government has an intervening role in families when there is an impact on others, especially children, and that this role was to 'support the casualties of marriage break-up', thus showing the government accept that the state has a role to play in insuring against life risks where children are concerned. The Child Support Act has reduced women's insurance from the welfare state when they meet a commonly occurring risk: poverty resulting from marriage or relationship breakdown. Now they are obliged to seek child support from an absent parent in most cases before being eligible for the full amount of a relevant benefit.

Smoothing Out The Level Of Income Over The Life Cycle

For many people affected by the Child Support Act, lone parenthood is not permanent, nor is the associated poverty. Most lone parents eventually find new partners and/or paid employment. But, even though there may well be later times of plenty during which they might 'replenish' the 'savings bank' of the welfare state, they encounter further difficulties in drawing support at a particular time of need, so that, continuing with this metaphor, one might say that 'credit' arrangements in this particular bank have become more stringent.

Stepping In Where The Family 'Fails' Or Cannot Provide Care Itself

Finally, the child support reforms will call on absent parents to meet the cost of family 'failure' individually. This will mean a reduction in the role of the welfare state to help out. Thus the financial burden of child care is seen more as a private matter than as a shared social responsibility in which we all have a stake, making divorce and the breakdown of a relationship more of a 'private trouble'. This is in tune with government policy not to provide state support for child care, making that also a private responsibility.

Conclusion

In conclusion, I would suggest that the Child Support Act has moved us further in the direction of a residual welfare state which acts only as a 'safety net'. It has reduced the scope for vertical redistribution and, to an ever greater extent, for horizontal redistribution.

Virginia Bottomley, in her 'The Family – Responding to Change' speech, 26 May 1994, in which she challenges as 'misguided' the 'golden age of the family' point of view, states:

> "Children need roots, need stability, need consistency and need security. Children need to be able to make sense of their lives. That is the constant role for families. It is a responsibility which they must continue to bear despite the economic and social pressures they face... Being a parent entails a long-term commitment."

This sentiment, in contrast with much of the 'back to basics' rhetoric of her colleagues, is one with which few would disagree. However, rather than fostering a welfare state or a child support system which would enhance families' efforts to meet those responsibilities, we have seen a set of child support reforms that is greedy, cynical and hypocritical, has not improved support for families in need, while at the same time creating hardship for others (absent parents and their families) all in the name of rolling back the state. Sadly, Mrs Bottomley continued in that speech:

"…It is the same principle which underpins the Child Support Act… Families are private institutions. Long may that remain."

Families may be private institutions but only partly. Families need support from society generally, particularly when facing difficulties. We can ill afford to withdraw it when the need for child support has never been greater. Poverty in families with children has reached new levels in both relative and absolute terms. If the Government were genuine in its claim that the Child Support Act is about making children come first, as was the title of its White Paper, and not the Treasury, then child support must be reformed as part of a package of reforms to tackle child poverty.

What is needed is for child support to be less Treasury-driven and for more parents with care — those who most need it — to have a share in the sums paid by absent parents. The Child Support Act has the capacity to provide much needed support to low income families, provided that the rules which govern its interactive effects with the social security system are less harsh and Treasury-driven. Now that further reform seems imminent, perhaps Government could introduce a relaxation in these rules. This might entail the introduction of a maintenance disregard for parents with care in receipt of Income Support, similar to the present earnings disregard. Or, parents with care on Income Support and the Treasury might be given an equal stake in maintenance collected by allowing parents with care to keep, without loss of benefit, some of the child support collected on their behalf, or perhaps a combination of the two in the form of a disregard plus taper as in the Australian system (on which ironically the UK legislation claims to be based).

Such measures could be tied with a more generous maintenance disregard or taper for lone parents who receive Family Credit, which takes more realistic account of the costs of working, including child care, and loss of housing benefit for owner occupiers. A guaranteed maintenance advance for women on Family Credit would also help reduce the uncertainty of income from child support and remove a significant work disincentive. But in order for any reforms to work, there must also be in place a far more effective collection and enforcement machinery by the Child Support Agency than we have seen in its first year.

In a recent interview (Brindle 1994, p.10), Alistair Burt, Parliamentary Under-secretary for Social Security with responsibility for the Child Support Act, claimed that the introduction of a maintenance disregard for parents with care on Income Support would cost the Treasury £150 million for each £5 foregone and would also act as a work disincentive. In Scotland, this estimate might get a 'not proven' verdict, since other evidence casts some doubt on the scale of the cost. An Institute for Fiscal Studies study published by the EOC (1994) estimated the cost of a £15 per week maintenance disregard for lone parents on income support as £135 million, with a further cost of £70 million to raise the maintenance disregard of those receiving Family Credit to £35 per week. Whichever estimate is closer to the truth, the cost might well be regarded as value for money if it actually reached children living in poverty. But such estimates may be excessive, since they could be substantially offset by lower recovery costs in collecting the child support in the first place. If all parents knew that child support being collected from absent parents actually reached and benefited their children, they might become a less resistant and more co-operative group. Such reforms could allow the Child Support Agency to work in partnership with parents. They could provide it with a political constituency that has an interest in defending its existence, and would be more significant and less divisive than further concessions to absent parents and their families. Changes such as these are needed which take greater account of how child support interacts with the wider means-tested social security system.

So I would not advocate scrapping the Child Support Act but strengthening it so that it realises its potential to achieve greater vertical and horizontal equity and to genuinely benefit those families the government claims it is aiming to help. We must continue to press for policies that recognise that child support is a joint responsibility, certainly of parents, but of society as well. Our collective future rests on children's current well-being. We need to see child support by families and the state, not as mutually exclusive alternatives, where one is withdrawn in equal measure as the other is introduced, but as complementary and working in partnership. Such an approach could be a start of a true 'back to basics' family policy of making 'children come first'.

References

Bradshaw, J & Millar, J. (1990), *Lone Parent Families in the UK.* London: HMSO.

Brindle, D. (1994), Alistair Burt Interview, *Poverty 88.*

Bryson, L. (1992), *Welfare and the State, Who Benefits?*, London: Macmillan pp.63-65.

Burghes, L. (1993), *One Parent Families: Policy options for the 1990s.* York: Joseph Rowntree Foundation.

Burghes, L. (1990), *One Parent Families*, London: Family Policy Studies Centre.

Child Support Agency (1994),*Child Support Agency: the first two years.* London: Department of Social Security .

Duncan, A., Giles, C. and Webb, S. [Institute for Fiscal Studies](1994), *Social Security Reform and Women's Independent Incomes*. Manchester: Equal Opportunities Commission.

Garnham, A. and Knights, E. (1994), *Putting the Treasury First*. London: Child Poverty Action Group.

Haskey, J. (1993), 'Trends in the numbers of one-parent families in Great Britain', *Popularion Trends*, 71, Spring.

Hills, J. (1993), *The Future Of Welfare: A Guide To The Debate*. York: Joseph Rowntree Foundation, November.

Holtermann, S. (1993), *Becoming a Breadwinner*. London: Daycare Trust.

Lister, R.(1994), 'Back to the Family: Family Policies and Politics under the Major Government', D Kavanagh & A Seldon, (eds.), *The Major Effect*. Macmillan.

Millar, J. (1992), 'Lone Mothers and Poverty', in Caroline Glendinning and Jane Millar (eds.), *Women and Poverty in Britain the 1990s*. Brighton. Wheatsheaf, pp. 149-161.

McKay, S and Marsh, A. (1994), *Lone Parents and Work: The Effects of Benefits and Maintenance*, [Policy Studies Institute]. London: HMSO.

Morris, S., Gibson, S. and Platts, A. (1993), *Untying the Knot: Characteristics of Divorce in Scotland*, Edinburgh: Central Research Unit, The Scottish Office.

OPCS (1993), *Census of Population 1991*. London: HMSO.

OPCS (1993), *General Household Survey 1991*. London: HMSO.

Roll, J. (1992), *Lone Parent Families in the European Community*. London: European Family and Social Policy Unit.

Wasoff, F. and Morris, S. (1993), 'The Child Support Act 1991 and Family and Civil Law in Scotland', *Journal of the Law Society of Scotland*, (December).

Wasoff, F. (1992), 'The New Child Support Formula: Algebra for Lawyers?', *Scots Law Times*, Vol. 40, pp. 389-392.

8

CREATING OUR FAMILIES' FUTURE

David Donnison

Introduction

THERE is no more urgent topic in Britain today than the future of our families. Along with many other western nations, we face a crisis which is inflicting great and growing hardships on our children and young people – hardships which ultimately damage all of us. This chapter begins with evidence for that statement. To respond sensibly to this crisis we need to understand its causes which are complex and wide-ranging. They are briefly outlined in the next section of the chapter. The third deals with the responses we should be making to the crisis, focusing particularly on the action which can be taken at the local levels where most of the people attending this meeting work. The chapter closes with some brief conclusions.

What We Are Doing To Children And Young People?

The dire statement with which this chapter began is not just the usual kind of grumble which more complacent people have come to expect from *Guardian*-reading progressives. We face a historic change, which is like nothing that has happened in this century or the previous one. Its worst effects are loaded onto children, young people and their parents. Much of the evidence about those effects is summarised by Richard Wilkinson in *Unfair Shares*, a report published by Barnardos in July 1994.

There has been a big increase in family breakdown and in the numbers of children being reared by one parent.

The numbers of children in public care under the age of 10 rose from 1985 onwards.

The proportion of children on Child Protection Registers set up by local authorities almost quadrupled during the 1980s.

Between 1986 and 1991 there was a dramatic increase in expulsions from school, for reasons of all kinds and among pupils in all age groups.

Several studies have shown that reading ages among 7–8-year-olds declined during the 1980s, regardless of the teaching methods used – a decline which was not universal but concentrated particularly at the lower end of the ability range.

One study suggests there has been a similar decline in mathematical attainment.

There has been a big increase since the mid-1980s in the numbers of homeless young people.

The numbers of drug offenders between the ages of 17 and 29 doubled between 1979 and 1989.

There was between a four-fold and a five-fold increase in the numbers of deaths from solvent abuse between 1980 and 1990.

Total reported crime – the majority of which is committed by young males – increased by almost 80 per cent and violent crime by 90 per cent between 1981 and 1991.

The suicide rate among young men aged between 15 and 24 increased by 75 per cent between 1983 and 1990.

In 1985 there began an increase in the mortality rates for men and women between the ages of 15 and 44 – the age group from which the parents of these youngsters are drawn. This increase cannot be explained by AIDS.

Some of these figures reflect changes in reporting practices, but there can be no doubt that hardships and stresses of many kinds, particularly afflicting children, young people and their parents, increased steadily through the early 1980s, and then much more dramatically after 1985.

These figures delineate the human effects – the statistically visible tip of a much more extensive iceberg – of growing poverty and inequality. If we accept the definition of poverty used by the European Union – the living conditions of those who have to survive on less than half the average income for households of their size in their country – then Britain, at the last count, had a larger number of its people in poverty and a bigger increase in this poverty than any other country in the Union. And this growth in poverty was loaded most heavily, not onto the single, the childless or the elderly, but onto families with dependent children – about 30 per cent of whom are now growing up in poverty.

That does not mean that the rest of us are unaffected. We help to pay the costs of keeping more and more families alive on social security and housing benefits, housing more people in prison, and treating more victims of poverty-related stresses through the health services. We pay higher insurance premiums for our houses and cars. Eventually it is the youngsters of today whose productivity, whose taxes and insurance contributions will pay our pensions. If they are ill-educated, untrained and unemployed, we cannot rely on their help in our old age.

More fundamentally, our growing social divisions blight the whole nation's hopes for the future. Nearly half this country's famous £50 billion deficit arises from the costs of maintaining the unemployed and the loss of the taxes which they would be paying if they were in work. While it persists every Chancellor will be fighting to cut public expenditure. With long queues of unemployed people waiting for every job in the lower reaches of the labour market, it is harder to get work for prisoners and for people with physical handicaps or learning difficulties, harder for students to work their way through college, harder for older people who would like to postpone retirement to do so. When so many people's jobs and mortgages are threatened it is harder for politicians to persuade them to respond generously to the needs of the poorest of their fellow citizens. The biggest change which has taken place in Britain during the last twenty-five years has been our loss of confidence in our capacity to work together to change things for the better.

The Forces We Contend With

Faced with these trends, progressives are prompted to explore economic and social causes and to devise policies which promise a fairer, less unequal society. Meanwhile more conservative people call for a revival of moral standards, and a rediscovery of the virtues of marriage and the two-parent family, saying it is time to understand a little less and to condemn a little more.

In reality, no such choice has to be made. It is of course important to strengthen relationships of order and mutual respect between parents, neighbours and citizens – the kind of relations which minimise family break-up, theft, violence, addiction and other destructive behaviour from which poverty-stricken neighbourhoods suffer most of all. And it is of course true that many of the poorest people live absolutely honest, orderly lives – just as it is true that some very rich people fail to do so. Nevertheless, the stresses inflicted by exclusion from the mainstream of one's own society and loss of hope for the future make that kind of order harder to maintain.

Many surveys have shown that crimes – and particularly crimes against property, which account for the majority of offences – tend to rise when consumption falls and when there is an increase in long-term unemployment. Other research shows that in neighbourhoods where few of the young men are in regular employment, fewer of the women in their age group get married and stay married. The sacrifice a woman makes in linking her life to a man's becomes less attractive if he cannot provide a regular wage packet in return.

When large numbers of lone parents are rehoused in bleak flats in remote estates with central heating systems which are impossibly expensive to run for anyone living on income support (and that too often happens) then – with the support of family and friends, or just because they are marvellously well-organised people – some of these parents will get by without infringing the law. But others will by-pass the electricity meters, or get a little job – or a little man – and conceal these things from social security officials, or go shoplifting to feed and clothe their children, or take to dealing in drugs … all of them criminal acts. And, knowing that so many of their friends and neighbours resort to these strategies for survival, all will become increasingly reluctant to be seen talking to police officers and other officials. Morality and community loyalties have not collapsed. The morality recognised in these communities becomes whatever behaviour is necessary to keep your child alive and well.

Everyone who has been a parent knows what is morally feasible in some circumstances may become quite unrealistic in others. When your five-year-old child comes home saying "I don't want to go to school any more: there's a boy who keeps hitting me and saying horrid things about me," do you say: "Pay no attention to him; make yourself some nice friends, and if he troubles you again talk to the teacher: I'm sure she'll sort it out"? Or do you say: "If he troubles you again, roll your fingers up like this to make your hand into a knobbly ball and hit him so hard that he learns to leave you alone"? You may prefer the more gentle response, but you cannot sacrifice your child to your principles. We all know there are some schools in which you would have to work collectively with parents and teachers to transform the place before your child could be expected to behave in non-violent ways.

Politicians and civic leaders would do better to work at creating a world in which it is easier for people to be good and less tempting to be bad than to lecture people on how they should behave. It is because moral standards are important that we have to attend to social circumstances.

To do that successfully, however, calls for an understanding of the complex trends now at work in western society. They have at least four dimensions, each interacting with the others. These can be briefly summarised.

First and most fundamental are the economic changes which began to work through the whole developed, capitalist world from about 1972 onwards. As the world's economy has become increasingly integrated, production of growing numbers of goods and services is moving to the more stable and better educated of the low-wage economies. Demand for the labour of less skilled people in the West has therefore declined. Wages in capitalist economies, which over the longer term used to move slowly towards greater equality, began to grow more unequal as those of workers in the lower third of the labour force fell further and further behind the rising incomes of those in its middle and upper reaches. Unemployment has risen, and more and more of those out of work are out of work for long periods – many of them effectively excluded from the work force for ever.

Today, unemployment in Britain is again falling, but the record of the last twenty years suggests, first, that we should fix our eyes on the 'non-workers' rather than the officially unemployed, because more and more people who would like a job have reclassified themselves as sick, early-retired or inactive. Trends in the numbers of non-workers are less hopeful than those for the officially unemployed. Secondly, experience suggests that, unless new policies are brought to bear, the numbers not working will 'bottom out' at a level higher than the previous trough and then rise to a new peak higher than the previous one.

These high levels of unemployment do not only damage the people who would like to work. They weaken the bargaining position of everyone in the lower reaches of the labour force: hence the deterioration in pay, security and working conditions at those levels of the labour market.

Thus far, the evidence deals with individuals, working or not working. But people live in households and their living standards and opportunities depend heavily on those of the households to which they belong. The second dimension of poverty emerges as soon as we look at households. More and more of them have two earners, and more and more have none. There are good reasons why that should be so – in family psychology (many couples find it difficult to accept that the woman will be the breadwinner), in the ways in which the lower-paid workers are recruited through local grapevines (if none of your family are working you are less likely to hear of job-opportunities), and in the working of the household means tests to which more and more people are subjected (as wages are driven down it becomes harder to find jobs which offer pay and security that are better than those provided by social security benefits).

These growing inequalities between households help to explain why we also have more house buying families and more homeless, more successful students and more excluded from school. It is the families with children who are most likely to be in poverty. There are three overlapping groups of them: low paid workers, lone parents, and the unemployed. Meanwhile, although some of the elderly, the single and the childless are having a hard time, most of them continue to make good progress.

People live not only in households but in neighbourhoods, and their opportunities depend heavily on the kind of neighbourhood it is. The third dimension of our growing poverty emerges as we turn to this scale of analysis. For many years the differences between regions and between city neighbourhoods in their incomes, housing conditions, employment levels and other measures of well-being grew smaller. That was the purpose of regional policies, urban renewal schemes and many other government programmes. But these differences are now opening out again. Great public housing schemes built to shelter industrial workers and their families were devastated when the industries closed and many of the more prosperous families moved out. Then public authorities, with their building programmes halted and increasingly desperate to find space for the homeless, for people coming out of long-stay hospitals and others with urgent needs, exacerbated the problems of these less popular estates by housing large numbers of the most vulnerable people in them without making any matching investment in management and support services.

Poverty in a neighbourhood where most people are poor is harder to bear than poverty in more fortunate areas: there are fewer job opportunities, fewer services – public and commercial – fewer and poorer charity shops and jumble sales. Schools and public transport are often poorer. Even the tomatoes cost more. It may be harder to get credit or to get short-listed for a job from an address in such places. Meanwhile the dangers of urban life arising from crime, traffic, pollution and other hazards are generally greater.

The fourth and most pervasive dimension of the stresses affecting families today is, in the most general sense, political – meaning that it arises from decisions in which power plays a part. Those influences operate at all levels. At the global scale it is fairly clear who will benefit most from the breaking down of tariff barriers and other restraints on international trade.

At the national scale the main causes of the sharp increase in poverty and inequality experienced in Britain since 1985 are not rising unemployment or impersonal economic forces but changes in taxes and in benefits, both of which have taken more from the poorer half of the population and given more to the richer half. When a Chancellor tells Parliament that rising unemployment is "a price well worth paying" to bring the economy back under control, he is not speaking to the unemployed but to the majority of the electorate who remain in work – the people whose inadequate productivity, excessive wage demands, insufficient savings, and excessive appetite for imported goods sent the economy out of control in the first place.

At the local level, our finding (in research upon Clydeside) that the most affluent suburb in the Region, with more graduates in its population than any other local authority in Britain and equivalent numbers of motor cars and public and commercial services, also has an excellent railway to the centre of town and more and cheaper bus services to the centre than the most impoverished of Glasgow's big housing estates, was not at all unusual. Such patterns are very common. Every Cleansing Department manager knows where the telephones will start ringing first if refuse collections are delayed. Every Chief Constable knows where neighbourhood watch schemes demanding more police attention will tend to form – in the areas where owner-occupation and car ownership are highest and crime is least common.

No conspiracy theory is needed to explain these patterns. Poverty starts from powerlessness, while wealth arises from – and confers – power, in commercial and administered market places alike. It's the way the world works. We need to be aware of that if we are to address problems of poverty effectively.

Mobilising A Response

The trends I have outlined, imposing growing hardships on children and their families, have not come to a halt. They are continuing, and degrading the whole of our society. Already, as Beatrix Campbell has remarked, "riots" have become "routine". Can we halt and eventually reverse these trends? And what contribution can people working at local levels make to that task? Every city and region is different and has to formulate its own responses. Here we can do no more than suggest some of the principles and priorities which may help them. Many of them are drawn from initiatives already to be seen in Scotland.

Much of the action required to contend with the basic economic trends which are throwing so many people out of work has to be taken at national and international scales. But many people and some whole neighbourhoods have now become so excluded from the mainstream that they will not find their way back unless special steps are taken at local levels to help them. The main elements of a strategy for that purpose – to be seen in some of the Scottish Partnership Schemes – are pretty well known. They include technical and confidence-building education, and child care which enables parents to participate in it. Where major investment in urban renewal or new building can be foreseen, every effort should be made to ensure that people who have been out of work for a long time get a share of the jobs to be created. This is often assumed to mean jobs in the construction industry, but that is a rough and fast-moving world in which it is difficult to find any security. While such opportunities should not be disregarded, more may be gained by looking for continuing jobs providing the services, public and private, which a new and more diverse population will need. This was one of the findings of a recent study of the benefits which people living in Craigmillar may secure from developments which are to take place in and around that Edinburgh housing scheme. But such opportunities cannot be seized without careful advance preparation and a good deal of political 'clout', together with a forecasting and planning capacity that impoverished neighbourhoods often lack.

Meanwhile it must be remembered that a lot of those who come to live in neighbourhoods where jobs are hard to find will be permanently or temporarily out of the labour force – pensioners, people with disabilities and some lone parents, for example. For them, it will be more important to ensure that they get all the social benefits to which they may be entitled than to create jobs and training. Experience gained in the Strathclyde and Lothian welfare rights services suggests that one of their rights workers should be able to secure well over £100,000 a year in additional benefits for the people whom they advise, and much of this money will be spent locally in ways which offer further benefits for people living in the area. Of all the public services, this is far the most cost-effective contributor to the economy of such areas. Social benefits redistribute, rather than create, wealth, but most of this money comes from the national, not the local tax payer.

Glasgow's programme for reducing dampness, improving insulation and heating systems and reducing fuel bills in council flats promises genuine gains for all concerned: warmer homes and more money to spend on food and clothing for the family, reduced rent arrears and fewer empty flats for City Housing, and jobs for local people.

The importance of giving a voice which cannot be neglected to the people who actually experience the problems to be tackled is now widely preached, if less often acted upon. There will normally be several different, and frequently conflicting, groups of widely varying political strength in any community of this kind. It will be impossible to hold a proper balance between them unless civic leaders take responsibility for that, and equip themselves with staff well prepared for the task. Mothers with young children are often the least well represented group in the meetings which community workers call: we have to take special care to ensure that their needs are not neglected. The community-based way of managing public services does not replace more traditional forms of public service; it makes them more complex, but potentially more effective.

Scotland has plenty of examples of good practice to offer. The Community Safety Initiative recently launched by Central Region and its Police force is one of them, involving a house-to-house survey and local community meetings to learn what dangers worry people most (giving different answers in each area), a big conference with community groups to discuss draft plans, and more intensive work with local people in the neighbourhoods with the greatest difficulties. One of the findings already emerging from this project is that fear and hostility between youngsters and older people living in the same impoverished areas are among the more destructive effects of our deepening social divisions.

These diverse projects will not add up to a coherent strategy unless they are informed by regular and comprehensive information about what is happening to our children and young people. That does not call for massive research. The data is already available in the files of the Health, Education, Housing, Police and Planning services – but in each case, usually, for different sub-areas, so that these services can never talk to each other about the same people, what is happening to them and what the services are doing for them. (However, Edinburgh is now bringing its administrative areas into coterminous form, although it will take a long time to get there.)

People should come to expect an annual report on the infant and maternal health and mortality, the housing conditions, the educational attainments, of their City's or Region's youngsters; the numbers excluded from school, or coming into public care; the numbers appearing before Children's Panels, becoming homeless, getting jobs or remaining unemployed ... and so on. They should be able to compare their youngsters' attainments with those of previous years, and with other Cities and Regions, and to identify the neighbourhoods and the ethnic groups whose families are suffering greatest stress or making best progress. This kind of report, monitoring the progress of a city's most important asset – its own children – will be far more useful than further data on dubious performance standards with which we otherwise become obsessed (houses built or vacant, medical operations and the waiting lists for them, examinations passed and failed...). It may also help to mobilise public concern more effectively than information about poverty, inequality and 'exclusion' which are all rather academic, middle-class concepts.

Such reports, coupled with a lively, community-based approach to family needs, will also remind us that special, one-off projects, focused on particular areas for limited periods of time, are a wholly inadequate response to the crisis in which so many of our children are involved. Even the Single Regeneration Budget, the latest – and in many ways the best – version of Whitehall's thinking about urban regeneration, still takes this form. We need permanent programmes and priorities, built into the budgets and practices of mainstream services, if we are to arrest and reverse the divisive trends of our times.

Conclusion

When Rowntree made his surveys of poverty in York – three times between 1899 and 1950 – he found many people having a hard time. But they were not excluded from the mainstream of their society to the degree that impoverished families can be today. They were struggling through the troughs of the lifetime cycle of alternating poverty and relative comfort experienced by all working class people. Solidly embedded in that class, with the help of the Labour movement and liberal forces in the middle class, they eventually achieved full employment, regulation of minimum wages and working conditions, and a welfare state which protected them from the worst hardships.

But today the lone parents, the families of the long-term unemployed and the intermittently employed, often living in bleak neighbourhoods with no job opportunities and few services, find that the political forces which used to be champions of the poor no longer speak for them but for the people who regulate them from the far side of various public service counters. The programmes and policies created with such struggle in the first half of this century are ill-equipped to tackle this new pattern of poverty effectively. Poor families themselves often see them as part of their problem, not part of its solution. The new patterns of public service now slowly taking shape in an attempt to reverse these divisive trends are not just an administrative reorganisation. They are a reassertion of the importance of local civic leadership, and an attempt to create a new politics of poverty capable of contending with new forms of social injustice.

References

Wilkinson, R. (1994) *Unfair Shares* Barnardos.

9

FAMILIES PAST AND PRESENT: VALUES AND MORALS

Ludmilla Jordanova

ALTHOUGH people have been reflecting on the history of the family for centuries, since the second world war this topic has come to absorb the energy of a significant number of professional historians. There are journals, organisations and conferences designed to promote historical work on the family. The prodigious growth of interest in the field prompts a number of questions: why are historians drawn to this topic, what kinds of approaches and sources do they use, are they generating insights of general interest, and what on earth do they mean by 'the family'? I shall try to address some of these questions in what follows, which is organised into six sections. In the first, I shall talk about some of the conceptual issues around the idea of 'the family' in order to suggest that it can only be understood if its cultural history is taken into account. Second, I shall outline some of the approaches historians have taken, in order to point out, albeit briefly, their advantages and disadvantages. Third, I shall discuss the sources available to historians, and again try to assess their value. Fourth, I will outline some of the major shifts that have been identified by historians of the family, in order to indicate something of the broad chronological patterns they have in mind. Fifth, I shall examine models of familial relationships – both in the past and now in use by scholars. Finally, I shall attempt to draw the threads together in a brief conclusion.

Concepts and Culture

The title of the conference did not in fact invoke the abstraction 'the family' but used its plural form. The distinction is important. 'Families' immediately makes us think of actual people, of the lived experience of just about everyone. 'The family' is an abstraction, which suggests something general, even global or universal, and this is made quite explicit in the very idea of there being an 'international year of the family'. It's not at all easy to unravel what is going on here. But whatever form is used the implication remains that there is something which is shared, throughout the world, because of family membership. At the same time we know that in practice this means very different things, not just from nation to nation, region to region, street to street, but even to members of the same family. There are, then, many assumptions concealed in the terminology we use, even if these are implicit rather than explicit. Furthermore, these assumptions have their own history, which needs to be revealed.

Sometimes a distinction is made between family history – genealogy, now one of Britain's most popular pastimes, and the history of the family – the professional study of both the qualitative and the quantitative aspects of marriage, child-bearing, household organisation, and related phenomena in the past. The genealogical enthusiasm for investigating where one came from, as evident in the pressures to trace blood relations following adoptions as it is in passion for tracing ancestry, is, of course, a historical phenomenon in its own right. We should note the very recent and dramatic increase in the use of local record offices by those studying their family histories. The interest in family trees is hardly new, although in earlier times it was predominantly a preoccupation of royal and landed people, but the manner in which we think about familial origins in the late twentieth century is markedly different from the ways in which this was done even one hundred years ago. The advent of new reproductive technologies and of international adoption, for example, are of growing importance for contemporary ideas.

Yet, our current assumptions about family life seem so common-sensical, they have become so thoroughly domesticated, that getting a critical distance from them is almost impossible. Naturally, lip-service is paid to cultural diversity, whether across time or space, but it is generally no more than this, I contend. The reasons are central to the points I want to make in this section of the paper. However we use terms such as 'families' and 'the family', the implication of universality is present. At one level we can simply say that these terms act as convenient umbrellas for many related phenomena concerning the organisation of intimacies, sexual and reproductive relations, consumption and production. At one level this is true, but it is also banal, or rather it is too superficial, since it does not ask why we connect these phenomena together, or how their sense of relatedness came about. It is possible to interpret these universalist assumptions in a somewhat different manner.

If the family is understood as a natural entity, then 'naturally' one would find it everywhere. One can sustain this position, which affirms the biological significance of human families, in a number of ways. The point I wish to make here is that it was at a specific historical moment, that is, during the eighteenth century, that the naturalness of the family, the idea that it was nature's most basic social unit, was first systematically asserted and explored. Accordingly, my argument runs, to understand current notions of 'family' we need to return at least to that period, and to assess the significance of this naturalization of the family. The possibility of certain kinds of social intervention depends in fact on the family being associated with general, biological properties. Nowhere is this clearer than in the concern with population, which first surfaced in recognisably modern form in political economy in the second half of the eighteenth century. Political economy saw itself as a science, more specifically a human science, and hence concerned with general phenomena in nature. It is no exaggeration to say that all philanthropic and state activity in relation to the family draws inspiration from either political economy or from its predecessor, political arithmetic. This was so because of the links between statecraft, vital statistics and the family as the source of nations' human resources that were beginning to be established in the seventeenth century. The notion, for instance, that there existed natural laws of population – current long before Thomas Malthus's famous *Essay on the Principle of Population* of 1798 –illustrates how a scientific approach to familial phenomena tapped into, and re-described, existing political concerns, while providing a fresh idiom for talking about what were already perceived to be 'problems' in relation to the family – above all, poverty and the wastage of children's lives.

Since our ideas of family are constructed in social and cultural contexts, and since these structure the way in which familial phenomena are actually experienced, the analysis of languages of kinship must occupy a central place in any account of historical change. In his splendid book *Keywords*, Raymond Williams suggested that 'family', the word, underwent an important shift in meaning in the late eighteenth and early nineteenth centuries. Previously, he claims, family meant household, so that servants and apprentices, who were an integral part of most domestic settings in the early modern period, could be spoken of as members of the family, not least since they, like its other members, were under the tutelage of the father/husband. By the middle of the nineteenth century, according to Williams, family meant only those related by blood or marriage, and hence in households with servants an upstairs/downstairs divide was linguistically affirmed, and the sense that family was a biological entity reinforced. If Williams is right, we may assume that the resonances of familial languages have changed markedly over time. However, it does not follow that all people use such languages in the same way at a given period or that they are unambiguous. One obvious contemporary example is the use of 'family' to mean specifically 'children', as in 'starting a family', at the same time as it can mean relations by blood and marriage, both lateral and by descent. While the context usually indicates which is meant, there is considerable variation in how many others are included when one speaks of one's family.

The multiple resonances of 'family' and the intense emotional investment in the term have a number of implications. One is that 'family' can be used, especially in political and moral discourses, in quite emotive ways. Mrs Thatcher, never one to miss tricks of this kind, was rather skilled in using it to evoke a sense of warm inclusiveness that actually veiled a highly moralistic and judgmental orientation to the ways in which people behave in their intimate relationships. This immediately alerts us to the potential of 'the family' to suggest a norm, an ideal model to which others should conform. The history of the idea of a Holy Family made up of Mary, Joseph and Jesus is particularly interesting in this regard. And it is striking that when families, or elements of them, are idealised, as they so often are, the notion of happiness is not far behind. Tolstoy captured this perfectly when he opened *Anna Karenina* with the sentence: 'All happy families are alike but an unhappy family is unhappy after its own fashion' (p. 13). The use of 'family' to evoke a mood of idealised happiness, or to reinforce norms, has a flipslide. Often we create a sense of what the family is about through negative definition, indeed for some commentators this is one of the functions of single parents and gay couples now. This phenomenon is not new; in the eighteenth and nineteenth centuries, the prostitute was a figure who was imagined as constituting a mortal, and moral, threat to the well-being of *proper* families. Hence, the prostitute as a social type helped, by exclusion, to define what such families should be like. What constitutes a *proper*, that is legitimate, family is always contentious; the history of the resulting struggles about legitimacy, both literally and more loosely, are extremely important.

Another way of expressing the point about the multiple resonances of 'family' would be to draw attention to the richness of metaphors of kinship. Marriage, for instance, is an extremely powerful image of union, while 'brother' and 'sister' have had a long and vigorous life in political contexts. Equally evocative are the terms 'motherly', 'maternal', 'paternalist', and 'patriarchal'. Indeed, the range of places in which ideas of kinship are central is so remarkable, that anyone interested in the ways societies work ignores this at their peril. It is for these reasons that I stress the need to understand the history of the family in cultural terms.

It is perhaps somewhat ironic that these complexities make life rather difficult for historians. I now wish to turn to a more detailed consideration of how they cope with them.

Historians' Approaches

In his influential book *Approaches to the History of the Western Family 1500-1914*, Michael Anderson argued that there were four principal historical styles used by historians of the family: first, those concerned with demography, whose emphasis, like his own, was on households, and on long term trends in births, marriages and death; second, those who foregrounded mentalities – the sentiments approach, who were interested in changing emotional relations and who emphasised social and cultural explanations; third, those who analysed family economies, for whom the main concern was the relationship between labour, household production and family consumption, and finally, those who used psychoanalytic approaches, and who could be safely dismissed. This is one possible schema, and although it has its limitations, it also has some merit. The limitations are that many historians have in fact combined these approaches in rather interesting ways, and that psychoanalytic orientations cannot be so lightly dismissed. The merits are that it draws attention to the novelty and influence of quantitative methods in history, since this is what has made the work on households stand out, and Anderson is right to point out that it is indeed a different enterprise to construct models of consumption and production (the first and third approaches) and to infer the quality of people's intimate relationships in the past (the second and fourth approaches). However, we could divide historians of the family into quite different categories. For example, and this goes to the heart of the matter, some historians claim that mentalities shift with demography, others that mentalities have remained more or less the same, even as the facts of life and death have dramatically altered. The classic instance is infant mortality: did parents grieve less for their children when the death of offspring was a common occurrence? Both positions can, of course, cite evidence in support of their case. The point is that these two historical approaches embody fundamentally different attitudes to human beings and assumptions about how they work. So do the four approaches mentioned by Anderson – these differences are not resolvable empirically by searching for more or better evidence, they go far deeper than that. This is important, because it should make present-day practitioners who work with familial issues seriously sceptical about the stability of historical understanding. What history has to teach, if anything, is unclear.

This is a complex matter, but it does serve to point up the need to deal with historical myths, such as the belief in the relatively recent demise of extended family forms, and to be alert to the possibility that the study of history can generate myths that serve specific purposes. Historians carry not only ideologies of the family, but their own baggage, which is at once personal and structured by their positions with respect to race, class and gender. We should, I think, be quite probing when it comes to historical knowledge, and we need to understand why, since the second world war, the family has become such a major field among professional historians. It will not be possible to give satisfactory answers to such questions here, but it may be helpful to make three points. First, it was very much under the influence of the social sciences that historians turned to the family. Second, it was also in reaction against the emphasis on high politics and diplomacy, which smacked of elitism, that they did so. Third, studying the family was a way of examining groups to whom relatively little attention had been paid – women and children – and making them legitimate objects of historical enquiry; that is, it expressed a political agenda. We may note that these professional and political agendas carried a price – until recently, for instance, very little historical work has been done on fathers and fatherhood, thereby perpetuating another myth that the family is the (private) domain of women, a notion that itself has a history. The current prevalence of the vocabulary of public and private, the assumptions about how these terms are gendered, and the current fashionable status of this topic are most significant, yet the model that underlies these debates flies in the face of so much of what we know about family, which has never in practice been a 'separate sphere' of private female domesticity.

I want to advocate a specific kind of scepticism about historical knowledge of the family, without suggesting that history is not useful. It is, but its usefulness entirely depends on an ability to understand and critically analyse its basic assumptions. I have already suggested that sources can be selected to meet the predispositions of the historian, while it is also true that working with particular kinds of sources affects the way the past is viewed. I shall now take this argument a little further.

Sources

I want to start my consideration of the kinds of evidence historians of the family have available to them by making two statements that may, at first sight, appear to be in tension with one another. First, virtually everything a society does is relevant both to the experience of family life and to representations of the family; hence there is a superabundance of source material. Second, many aspects of family life were not recorded in the past because they were so ordinary, so taken for granted and so ubiquitous that there was no reason why they should be. Both these claims seem to me to be true and important. Let's examine the first in a little more detail. The range of sources available to us is indeed huge, especially if we include art, music, literature, architecture, costume and so on along with the full range of archival and printed sources historians customarily use. In order to make effective use of such sources we need to think about how they were produced. To put it crudely and over-simply, most were produced by elites of one kind or another; accordingly, when the mass of the population is represented in such sources, they tend to come in through the eyes of other classes with whom they had, to say the least, ambivalent relationships. Even sources that appear to come straight from popular experience should be treated with care. The best example of this is the use of trial records, and especially statements by witnesses, which were, for many periods, not the unmodified, authentic voice of the people that historians have sometimes supposed them to be. The fact that this vast range of sources has certain 'distortions' built into it, does not mean it is without value. How the dominant groups within a culture represent the family is a matter of some significance. To take a contemporary analogy – we can learn a great deal from advertising about images of gender, parental and sexual relationships, while at the same time we recognise that such images do not reflect in any unproblematic way the way things are. On the contrary, advertisers' images are created by powerful interests, they have a normative element, they often idealise intimate relationships, they manipulate viewers' feelings quite unashamedly, but the precise ways in which they do so afford powerful insights into contemporary culture.

My second statement recognises that, especially in the past, there was no mechanism for, or perceived need to record, many aspects of daily life. What is quotidian may be accidentally recorded, but is rarely systematically set down unless for legal reasons – inventories, financial transactions, and so on. In the wealth of available sources, there are, then, striking lacunae. My contention is that this is a quite significant phenomenon when it comes to children, and perhaps I can illustrate the point through the example of child labour – an emotive subject about which surprisingly little is known historically. In one of its forms – its organised manifestation in apprenticeship – we know a certain amount, but this is the exception rather than the rule if we take eighteenth-century England as an example. Most of the 'information', if it can be called that, comes from those who wanted the practice regulated. Yet, historians of the nineteenth and twentieth centuries are now discovering how fully integrated child labour was into the fabric of working-class life. Of course, it is important to think about how child labour should be defined. I suspect that we, following the philanthropists of the late eighteenth century onwards, associate it above all with hard physical work outside the home, but this may be anachronistic. Furthermore, a romanticised picture of family life in the past is often implied, where somehow a communal endeavour for the good of all (children working on small-holdings, in the home, with siblings) is given a benign moral valence, but 'alienated' child labour (in factories, mines and so on) is not. While there are many reasons for this, the nature of the sources plays an important part. In the absence of details of how work and family dovetailed, we find it difficult to generate a richly-textured image. Given the superabundance of wonderfully written, nakedly emotional sources condemning child labour, we can with ease imaginatively nurture a sense of its moral iniquities.

This point about how the available sources affect historians' imaginations is worth bearing in mind when we consider the huge influence that demographic studies of the family have had. Scholars have clung onto whatever quantitative sources are available to them, for obvious reasons, but two difficulties result. First, there is a tendency to extrapolate feelings from vital statistics, as if knowing the latter leads inexorably to knowing the former. As my earlier example about the prevalence of child death was intended to illustrate, it does not necessarily follow that because more children died young parents adapted by loving them less or by inuring themselves against grief – some may have done, many, we know, did not. Nonetheless, the temptation to make quantitative sources bear more interpretation than is strictly legitimate is strong. Second, in building models based on demographic data, assumptions are made about the basis upon which human beings act. The material interests of individuals and communities are taken to be paramount, to be capable of regulating age of marriage for economic reasons, for example. The magnitude of the claims implicit here is clear from the fact that early modern, pre-Malthusian, communities had rather low levels of illegitimacy, despite high average ages of marriage, suggesting that young people did regulate their sexuality in an age when effective mechanical birth control was unknown. This strikes me as posing a challenge to historians to imaginatively reconstruct the psychic, cultural and social mechanisms by means of which such sexual and reproductive regulation took place. In practice, it is just assumed that they do take place in some uncomplicated manner. Interestingly enough, this historical approach fits with at least some of the styles of thinking in early political economy, which was among the first attempts to theorise demographic trends. Thomas Malthus, who did not believe people found it at all easy to regulate their sexual desires, basically understood population in terms of individual and collective interests.

Historians have many professional responsibilities, not only to the scholarly community that they serve, but to a wider public. Working out how to meet those responsibilities is not at all easy, and is something we fail to pay enough attention to. Surely we must seek ways of understanding the past that do justice to the complexities of human experience. The tenor of my argument has been to suggest that this involves an imaginative engagement with our forebears; since historians both identify with and distance themselves from their objects of study, I cannot see how the psychic dimension can be ignored. My aim in this section has been to suggest that the kinds of sources selected and the ways they are treated and interpreted inevitably affect our vision of families in the past.

Similar arguments apply to periodisation, which is used to impose a meaningful shape on the messiness of past time, and these shapes are dense with assumptions, less perhaps about human nature than about how our modern world has been forged. I turn now to chronology and periodisation.

Patterns in Time

Many works have been written on the theme of the 'making of the modern family'. Most of these see the eighteenth century as a crucial period of transition. This is generally sustained in two distinct ways. First, it is claimed that the *quality* of family relationships changed from a more formal mode into a more overtly affectionate loving one. Evidence for this is derived from the ways in which spouses are chosen – less, it is claimed, by parents, more by the participants themselves, more for 'love' – and also from changes in parent/child relationships, which allegedly became closer, more direct and affectionate, less stilted and less mediated through servants. While I have necessarily presented this very briefly, I believe it conveys something of how the transition is presented even in the work of distinguished historians like Lawrence Stone. The obvious points to make concern the class basis of such claims, which is connected with the kinds of evidence available, the difficulty of inferring the quality of intimate relationships from the sources, and the implausibility of even all elite groups undergoing such changes even vaguely in tandem. It is significant that in so many historical works and in not a few general ones, a grand narrative of our civilisation has become the merging of romantic love, including a sense of the romance between parents and children, with family life. The underlying assumption is that all kinds of fulfilments, above all sexual ones, are now to be found, with all the norms that implies, in recognisably familial structures. This grand narrative draws on supposed historical evidence to serve quite other ends, to sustain myths about late twentieth-century Western societies that are at best insidious and at worst dangerous.

The second way in which the idea of an eighteenth-century transition to the modern world has been sustained yokes together the industrial revolution, women's work and family life. The key idea is that as women in particular entered a waged economy *as individuals*, their sense of themselves changed, they became more sexually autonomous and hence more active subjects in other ways – in the family, politically and so on. This thesis has been put in a most extreme form by Edward Shorter, who is, to say the least, a controversial historian. Ultimately he wants to argue that feminism becomes possible once women have control over their own bodies, and this only occurs when medicine can provide secure methods of birth control and safe child bearing. For Shorter, this happened over the nineteenth and twentieth centuries, although the groundwork for this individualism was laid at the end of the eighteenth century. While it has been easy to poke fun at Shorter, the fact remains that here too is a grand narrative to which many people subscribe, especially those concerned about population growth, who see enhancing women's economic, political and sexual autonomy as a, if not the, major way of effecting changes in family life, which will in turn lead to fewer children.

There are at least two other ways in which the story about modernising the family can be told. (In addition there is the one mentioned earlier about the loss of the extended family in favour of the nuclear family, but I shall not be concerned with that here.) The first derives from a legal framework, and charts shifts in family life in terms of legislative change. This is a story about the increasing rights of family members as individuals. It is possible, for instance, to build a narrative around the Hardwicke

Marriage Act of the mid-eighteenth century, the advent of civil registration and divorce in the mid-nineteenth century, the married women's property acts and the widespread provision of education at the end of the century, and so on. Indeed historians often grasp at legislation as a way of providing themselves with a supposedly solid framework. Legislation does not necessarily reflect general values and concerns, nor does it always have its intended effects, its actual impact is notoriously hard to chart, takes place often unevenly and over long periods of time. Perhaps most important of all perhaps in relation to the family is the fact that there are many parts the law simply does not reach – which means that what can be inferred about either attitudes or arrangements in the populace more generally is severely limited.

In the situation in which we find ourselves, legislative change and the role of the state in relation to the family seem to be natural partners, walking hand in hand. But I want to separate them here, since the story that is often told of changes in the family by virtue of the role of the state does not depend on legislation, or even on national trends. In the search for clear ways of periodising change, the involvement of the state has appealed because it fed a widespread feeling in many Western countries since the second world war, either that a mighty and intrusive political apparatus existed that had to be resisted or that the core of what was socially useful about the family was being reinforced and defended by the state. These are simply two sides of the same coin, while the moral tone is different, the grand narrative that links family and state remains essentially the same. It is perhaps significant that this theme has been more important for Continental historians than it has for British ones, but even in relation to Britain, it has structured our sense of how the professions, above all medicine, have made an impact upon family life. Many shifts in medicine in the eighteenth and nineteenth centuries – the rise of man-midwifery, then obstetrics and gynaecology, the development of general practice, eugenics, vaccination and so on – may be connected with changes in family life. The concomitant assumption is that doctors were agents if not directly of the state at least of its values, that they inserted political values into the domestic arena. One can tell the family-state-medicine story in a number of ways, according to ideological preference; for example, either doctors controlled women's reproduction and sexuality on behalf of the state, or, doctors were women's allies, helping them control their own bodies.

Just as important, however, have been the local political forces that shaped family life. In earlier periods it was forms of philanthropy and the operation of poor relief by parishes. Once this has been recognised, the grand narratives around state intervention and the family have to be modified, and this in turn suggests a different chronology, with intervention, at least in some forms, coming much earlier.

My aim in this section has been to indicate some of the ways in which historians think about shifts in relation to the family over the last three hundred years or so, and to illustrate some of the assumptions they carry with them. These assumptions, like others I am drawing attention to in this paper, are closely bound up with what I will call familial models, and it is to this topic that I now turn.

Models of Family

I have already made it clear that historians deploy complex models of the family and human nature, even if they are not fully conscious of doing so. All societies, it seems to me, operate with models of kinship. In the recent history of Western families several have been in operation at any one time. These are images of the family as a whole which inform, in quite profound ways, what can be thought in relation to 'family'. The analogy between family as microcosm and the state as macrocosm would be a good example. 'Little commonwealth', 'miniature fatherland' – these ideas of the family remained current into the nineteenth century, as Davidoff and Hall have shown. Other models include the family as the unit for the transmission of property, for raising children, for organising patronage networks. Just as important are models of constituent relationships within the family – parents and children, husband and wife, between siblings, and with more extended kin. These models are historically specific and provide important clues to responses to families and perceived changes within them. An illustration may be in order here. Eighteenth-century commentators waxed lyrical about breast-feeding and sought to persuade, especially aristocratic women, to give up their wet-nurses and feed their children themselves. This much is well-known and all the credit, if that is the right word, given to Rousseau. In fact, there was quite a widespread movement around this issue; it opened up the possibility of imagining the essence of the mother/child relationship being in the act of breast feeding. This further allowed people to imagine that, since the breast was associated with desire between men and women, it served to bind together members of the human family, itself seen as the natural unit upon which society was based. The model of family and of mother/child bonding that is implicit here was taken up in many different forms, especially in the visual arts, where the Madonna as lactating mother served as an antecedent. These models were explicit vehicles for moral values – as we know from our own time, attempts to idealise certain kinds of motherhood, and to demonise others have real political bite and they rest on models of constituent family relationships. These models have two properties I wish to draw attention to: first, although elements of them have been remarkably persistent, they are historically produced in ways that require systematic exploration; second, they have considerable power, not least because they are part of structured ideologies.

Conclusion

I want to conclude by rephrasing the arguments I have made here under six points.

1. I am sceptical about drawing direct lessons from history. Nonetheless, there are productive ways of thinking about the family to be drawn from historical writings, especially an understanding of the cultural placement of thinking about and images of the family.

2. In order to put such understanding to good use we need to distinguish between those bits of societies that are concerned with the family on a more systematic, general and abstract basis, and the ways in which actual families experience themselves. Of course there are connections between these, but they are far more tangled than is usually supposed. In each case somewhat different sources and approaches are required. I have implied that it is illusory to suppose we can know the reality of family feelings in the past, and that we need to watch out for the myths that can masquerade as secure historical knowledge and to be alert to the interests they serve.

3. More particularly we need to understand how knowledge about the family has been and is being produced, largely within the social sciences. This knowledge has a history, and a sociology, which needs to be comprehended in order to evaluate it. In other words, the history of the family must include the history of the areas that study the family, of how knowledge about it is produced. In effect this is a plea for more reflexivity, which means treating history more as a consciousness-raising discipline than as a mine of information.

4. Historical perspectives can show particularly effectively the special senses in which the family is political – this is the point I have been making throughout, that 'family' necessarily suggests 'values and morals', which always concern relations of power, that is, politics with a little p, and that family is also about Politics with a big P, in ways that historical examples can satisfyingly illustrate, when contemporary matters are too close to home. Historians can reveal why the politics of the family always seems fresh and urgent, even when its preoccupations are palpably not new.

5. The power of idealisations is an illustration of this point – idealisations of certain kinds of family, and of specific familial qualities/relationships have been of huge significance. I would argue they are of greater importance now than they were in the past. Idealised visions of the family are artificial and simplified – they grip people, and, at the same time, serve to point up the extent to which daily life does not, cannot, fit

with them. Such idealisations come out of social/cultural structures. Historians can help develop ways of understanding a phenomenon of outstanding potency in contemporary life.

6. To speak of the future, of my utopian aim, is perhaps to exceed my brief as a historian, but in gaining a better purchase on the dominance of familial languages and images in conceptions of human relationships, we might perhaps be inspired to imagine other ways that are apt for our time and for the future. We know how rigid and constraining notions of family have been in the past – perhaps a first step towards their not being so in the future. Is it too paradoxical for a cultural historian of the family to suggest that those who are interested in its future might pay as much attention to new reproductive technologies as to demography, that they might be as concerned with science fiction as with the law, as interested in advertising as in education?

References

Anderson, M. (1980) *Approaches to the History of the Western Family 1500-1914.* Macmillan.

Casey, J. (1989) *The History of the Family.* Oxford.

Davidoff, L. and Hall, C. *Family Fortunes: Men and Women of the English Middle Classes 1780-1850.* Routledge.

Donzelot, J. (1980) *Policing the Family.* Macmillan.

Gay, P. (1985) *Freud for Historians.* O.U.P.

Pollock, L. (1983) *Forgotten Children : parent children relations from 1500-1900.* C.U.P.

Scarre, G. (ed).,(1989) *Children, Parents and Politics.* C.U.P.

Shorter, E. (1976) *The Making of the Modern Family.* Collins.

Shorter, E. (1987) *A History of Women's Bodies.* Basic Books.

Stone, L. (1990) *The Family, Sex and Marriage in England.* Penguin.

Strathern, M. (1992) *After Nature: English Kinship in the Late 20th Century.* C.U.P.

Tolstoy, L. (1939) *Anna Karenina* translated by L. and A. Maude. O.U.P.

Williams, R. (1976) *Keywords : a vocabulary of culture and society.* Fontana.

10

CONCLUDING REMARKS: FAMILIES AND THE FUTURE

Stewart Asquith and Anne Stafford

AS mentioned earlier, there was some disappointment expressed at the conference on which this book is based that no announcement had at that time been made regarding a Children Bill for Scotland. Given the number of reports on child and family matters which had been produced in Scotland in previous years and the publication of the White Paper *Scotland's Children* in August 1993 a degree of optimism had prevailed that such a Bill was imminent and would have wide-ranging implications for families in Scotland in the future. An integrated Children Act had been introduced in England and Wales in 1989 and the lack of such a legislative framework for Scotland was seen as an omission.

However, on the 24th November, 1994, a Children (Scotland) Bill was indeed introduced into parliament. At the time of writing, the full implications of the Bill are still being considered but it is such a significant element in the process of the review of child care law in Scotland that a brief statement of the main proposals contained in it is presented here. Kathleen Marshall (Chapter 4) did of course address crucial aspects of what were anticipated to be the changes in child care introduced by a Children Bill for Scotland. We merely record here what in fact some of the proposed changes are.

The Children (Scotland) Bill is of course based largely on recommendations and proposals contained in the various reports which were published in Scotland in recent years. These included of course, the *Child Care Law Review* (1990), the Reports on the Orkney and Fife Inquiries (1993), the *Study of the Role and Functions of Children's Reporters* (Finlayson Report 1992), *Review of Residential Child Care*, Scottish Law Commission's *Report on Family Law* (1992) and the first published paper (1992) of the *Review of Adoption Law in Scotland*. The White Paper *Scotland's Children* had outlined the Governments proposals for policy and law relating to children derived largely though not exclusively from the recommendations of the earlier reports.

Influential in the whole process were key principles drawn from the United Nations Convention on the Rights of the Child with an explicit commitment to these contained in *Scotland's Children*. The very first recommendation of the Clyde Report had been that change in child care law and policy should be informed by the philosophy and principles of the UN Convention on the Rights of the Child and with the publication of *Scotland's Children* and the Children (Scotland) Bill, the rights of children underpins many of the changes recommended. But as a reading of the UN Convention reveals, the responsibilities of parents and the importance of support for families are also identified as significant factors in improving child care law, policy and practice. The wide ranging scope of the Children (Scotland) Bill has important implications not simply for child care but for family life in general and, as Ian Lang stated in launching the Bill, "it seems fitting that such an important and extensive Bill is being introduced during the International Year of the Family".

One of the criticisms made of the current state of child care law in Scotland is that it is fragmented, confusing and difficult for children and families to negotiate. Along the lines of the Children Act in England and Wales, the Bill seeks to integrate existing legislation in a comprehensive and coherent statement:

> "One of the most significant aspects of the Bill is its scope. It emphasises the responsibilities which parents have in raising their children, but also clearly sets out what rights parents have to enable them to fulfil these responsibilities. Importantly, it stresses that both parents should have a continuing role to play in the upbringing of their children, even after separation or divorce. The Bill will maintain and strengthen the Children's Hearings system based on the principles of the Kilbrandon Report for the care of children. It will introduce new child protection measures and place wider duties on local authorities to promote the welfare of children"(Secretary of State for Scotland 1994).

One of the key principles drawn directly from Article 12 of the UN Convention on the Rights of the Child and embodied in Part I of the Bill is the importance given to the views of children being taken into consideration in any major decision affecting their lives. This relates to decisions by persons with parental responsibilities, the making of court orders, the reaching of decisions at children's hearings, children in care of the local authority, the making of exclusion orders and any decision relating to adoption. But similarly Article 3 of the Convention privileges the interests of the child and the Children (Scotland) Bill likewise emphasises the importance of the welfare/interest of the child (see clauses 1, 11 (5) (a), 17 (1) (a), 16 (1) and 83). Part I also states the responsibilities and rights of parents as regards their children. The concepts of 'custody' and 'access' are replaced with concepts of 'residence' and 'contact' allowing children to maintain personal relations and direct contact with both parents.

Part II of the Bill transfers most of the provisions relating to children from the Social Work (Scotland) Act 1968 to the Children (Scotland) Bill with the overall intention of making child care law more coherent and understandable to all those concerned. Local authority social welfare responsibilities towards children are enhanced in general with local authorities, amongst other things, required to publish plans for services to children (clause 18), to produce information for services for children with and affected by disabilities [20 (4)]. Part II also makes a number of changes to provisions for the Children's Hearings system and repeals almost all of Part III of the Social Work (Scotland) Act 1968. In particular, children's hearings are to have a greater degree of specification in making supervision requirements; parents, relevant persons and the press can be excluded from hearings where this is in the interests of the child [Clauses 37 (4), 38 and 40 (1)]; there is to be an extended role for safeguarders (35); there are to be a number of new orders with the objective of protecting children including Child Protection Orders(51, 53, 55, 57 and other clauses), Child Assessment Orders (48), Exclusion Orders(67–71); and a new Parental Responsibilities Order (Clauses 76–78).

Part III makes a number of specific amendments to the Adoption (Scotland) Act 1978.

The Children (Scotland) Bill presents the first major review of child care in Scotland since the introduction of the 1968 Social Work (Scotland) Act and presents a comprehensive framework for the development of child care law, policy and practice. Though fuller analysis of the proposal for change is still required, most will be welcomed by the community of individuals in Scotland charged with a responsibility for children. There are however, notable omissions. For example, there has been a growing lobby in the United Kingdom for some form of Child Welfare Commission which would both monitor and enhance policy and practice developments impacting on the lives of children. From a Scottish perspective, the Child Care Law Review had raised the issue as long ago as 1990 and a number of commentators since have identified the potential of a Child Welfare Commission for the enhancement of the lives and experiences of all children.

Also, the position as regards the use of corporal punishment on children has been left somewhat vague and lacking in clarity since the Scottish Law Commission produced the Report on Family Law in 1992. Recent decisions in England & Wales allowing child minders the right to smack children have further complicated the issue and it had been hoped by certain sections of the community that a clear statement against the use of physical punishment on children would have been made.

Nevertheless, the Children (Scotland) Bill will undoubtedly have important implications for Scotland's children and families in the future.

The proposed changes in child care and child law hold significant repercussions not just for children but also for parents and family life in general. The social, political and economic status of children is currently being reappraised in light of the United Nations Convention on the Rights of the Child. As notions of children, childhood and children's rights alter, there are likewise important changes required in how we as adults relate to children and in the nature of the experiences afforded to them within the family, by our major social institutions and in society in general. The Children (Scotland) Bill is an important part of the whole process of change which should ultimately lead to a better future for families.

However, it would be wrong to assume that change in the legislative framework relating to children would in itself produce a dramatic alteration in the nature of the life experiences of many of our children. As many of the contributors to this volume emphasise, the future for many children and their families is one in which they will experience poverty and all the other factors associated with it. As the gap between the rich and the poor widens, extending the effects of social inequality, the future for many families and their children is a bleak one. More than rhetoric will be needed to effect change in that.

INDEX

HMSO publications are available from

HMSO Publications Centre
(Mail, fax and telephone orders only)
PO Box 276, London, SW8 5DT
Telephone orders 071-873 9090
General enquiries 071-873 0011
(queuing system in operation for both numbers)
Fax orders 071-873 8200

HMSO Bookshops
49 High Holborn, London, WC1V 6HB
(counter service only)
071-873 0011 Fax 071-873 1
68-69 Bull Street, Birmingham, B4 6AD
021-236 9696 Fax 021-236 9699
33 Wine Street, Bristol, BS1 2BQ
0117 92643060Fax 0117 9294515
9-21 Princess Street, Manchester, M60 8AS
0161-834 7201 Fax 0161-833 0634
16 Arthur Street, Belfast, BT1 4GD
01232 238451 Fax 01232 235401
71 Lothian Road, Edinburgh, EH3 9AZ
0131-228 4181 Fax 0131-229 2734
The HMSO Bookshup
The Friary, Cardiff CF1 4AA
01222 395548 Fax 01222 384347

HMSO's Accredited Agents
(see Yellow Pages)

and through good booksellers

Printed in Great Britain for HMSO Scotland by
CC No 20249 IOC 6/95